Geometric Pattern Coloring Book

This book belongs to :

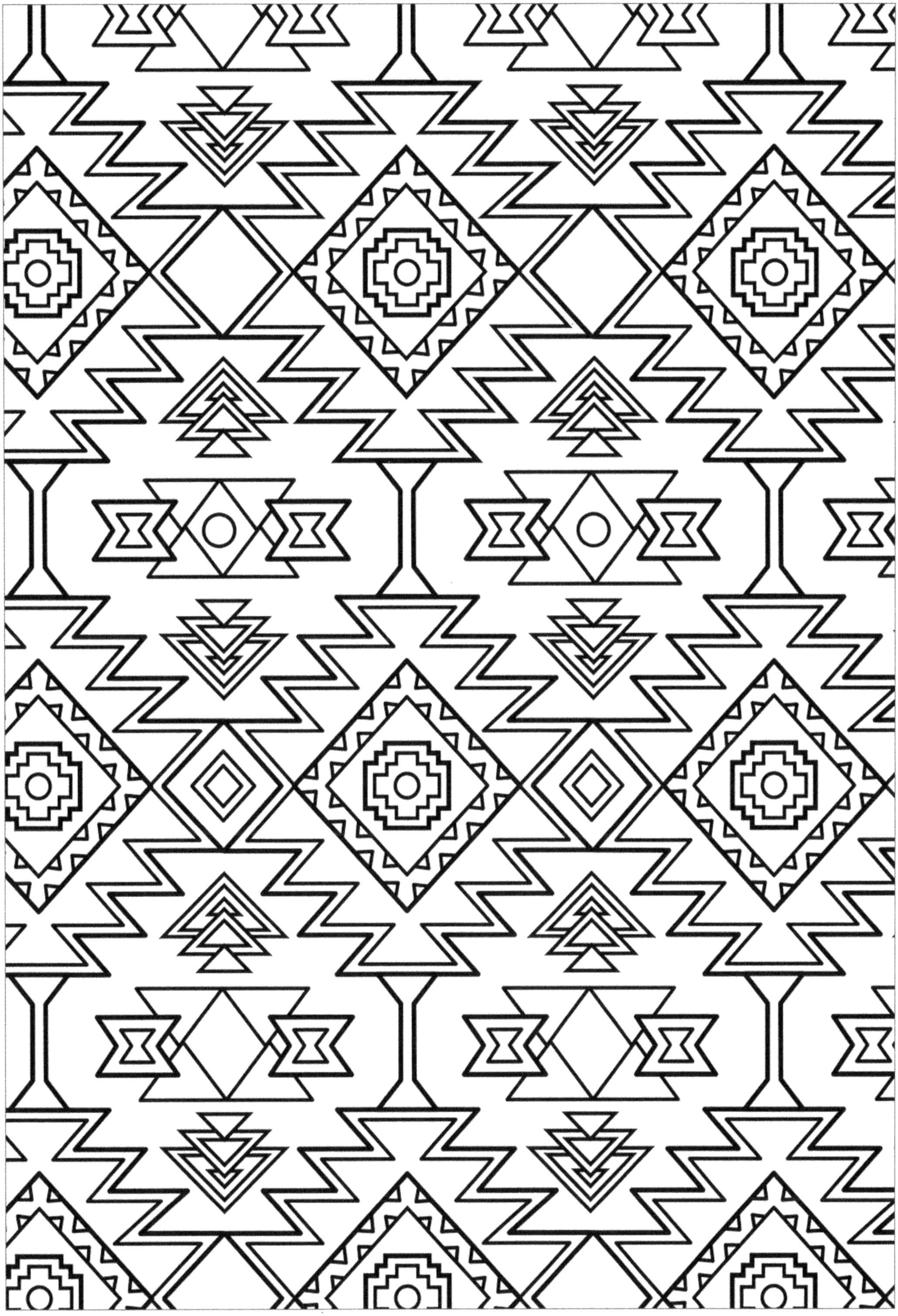

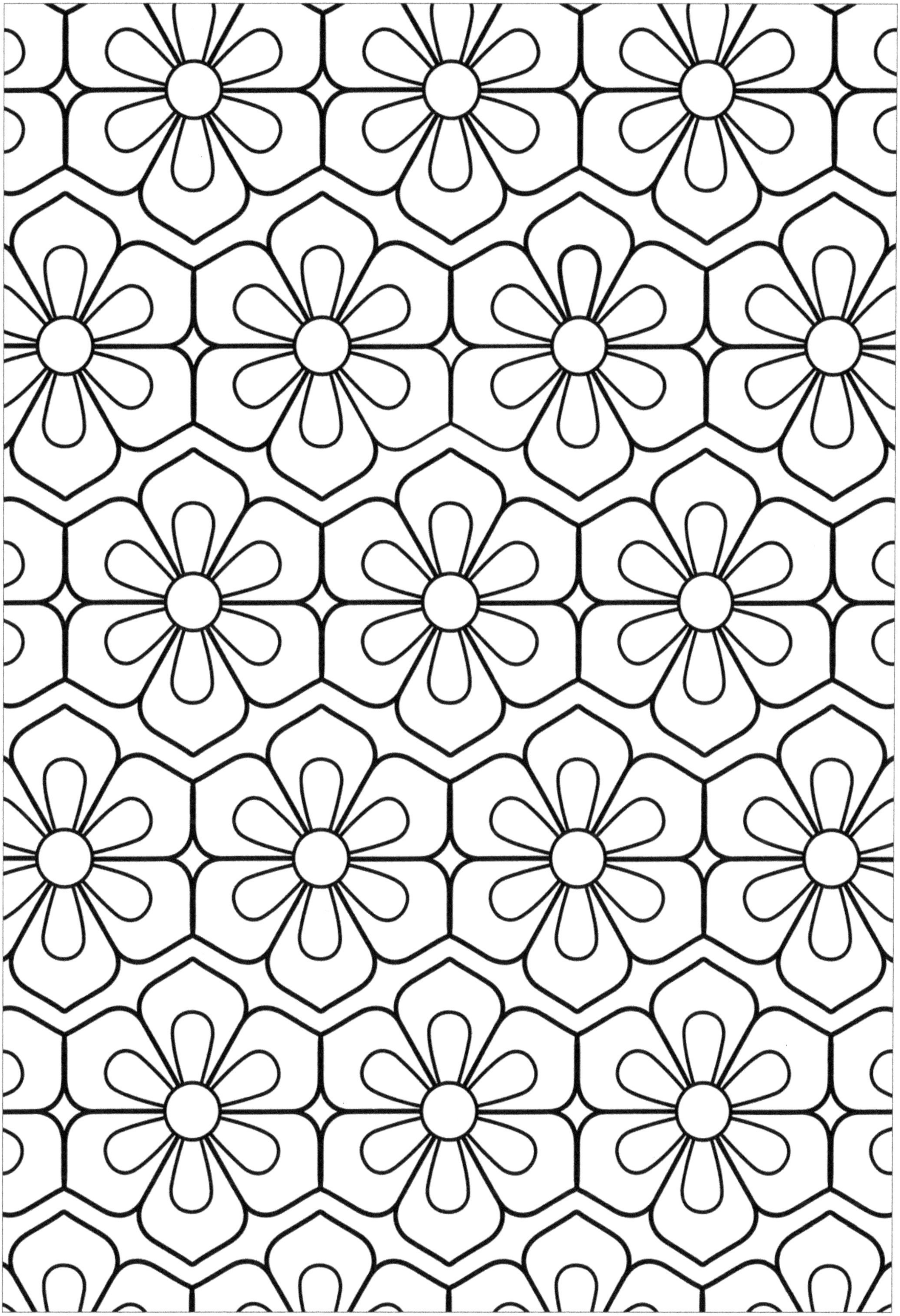

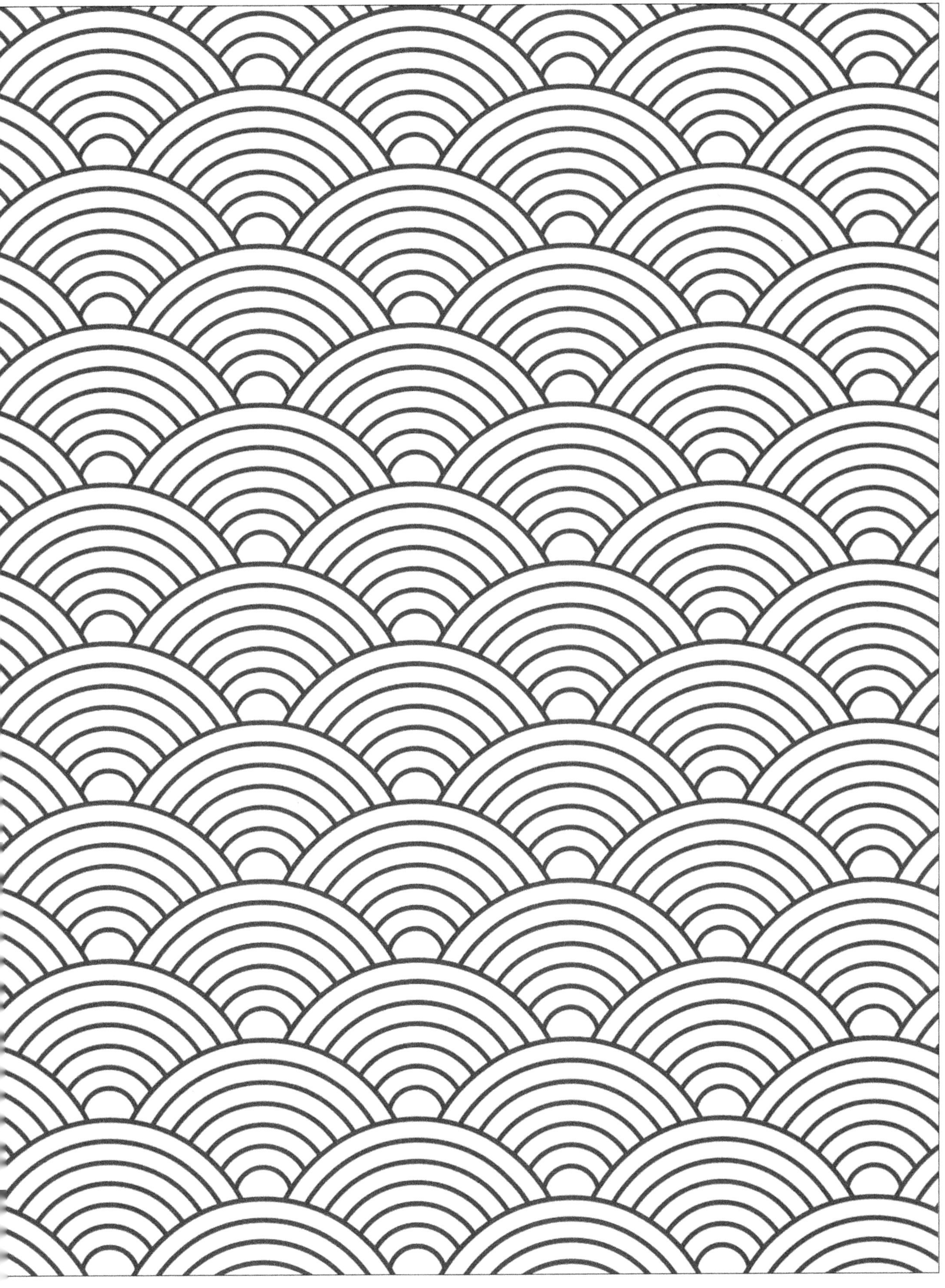

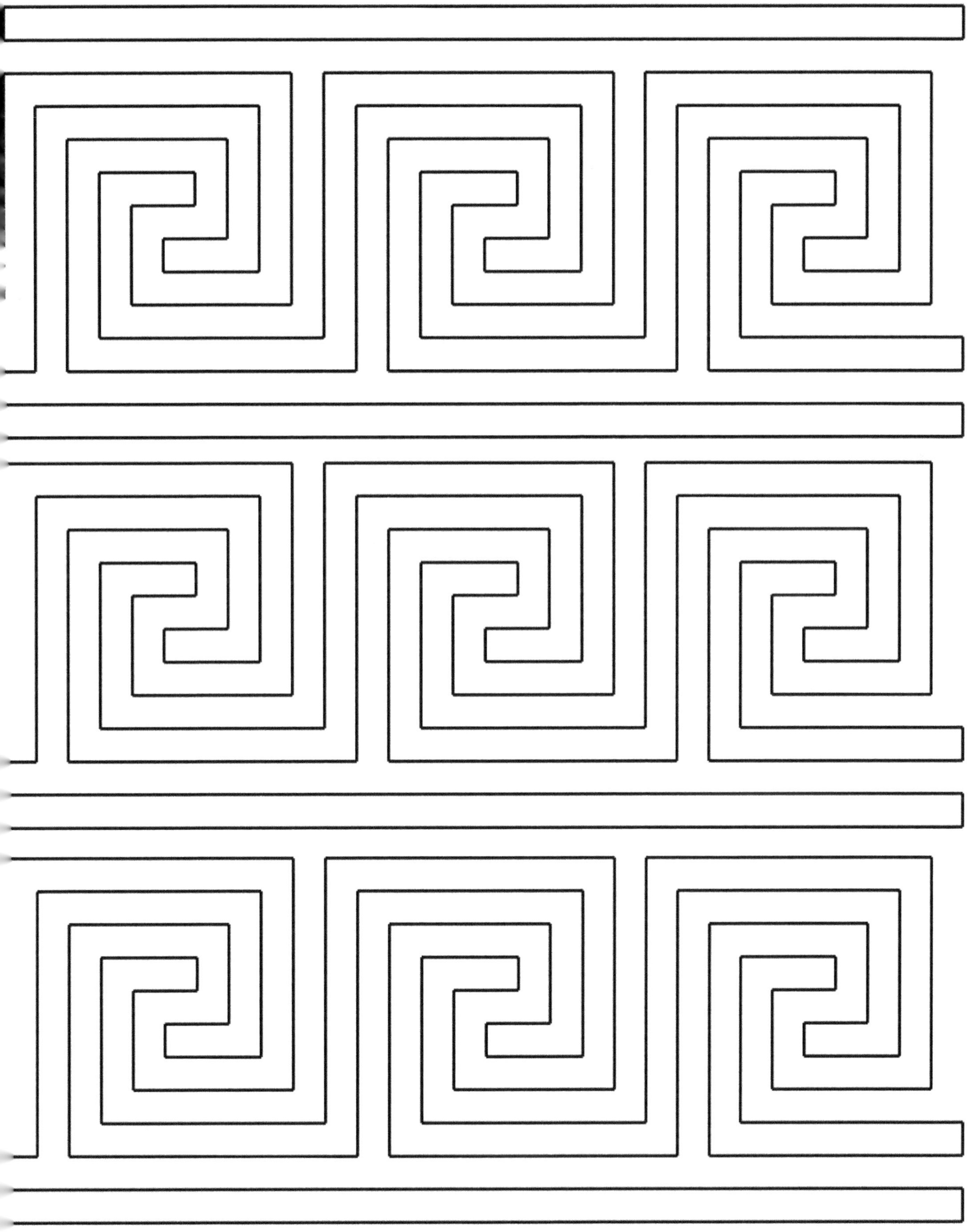

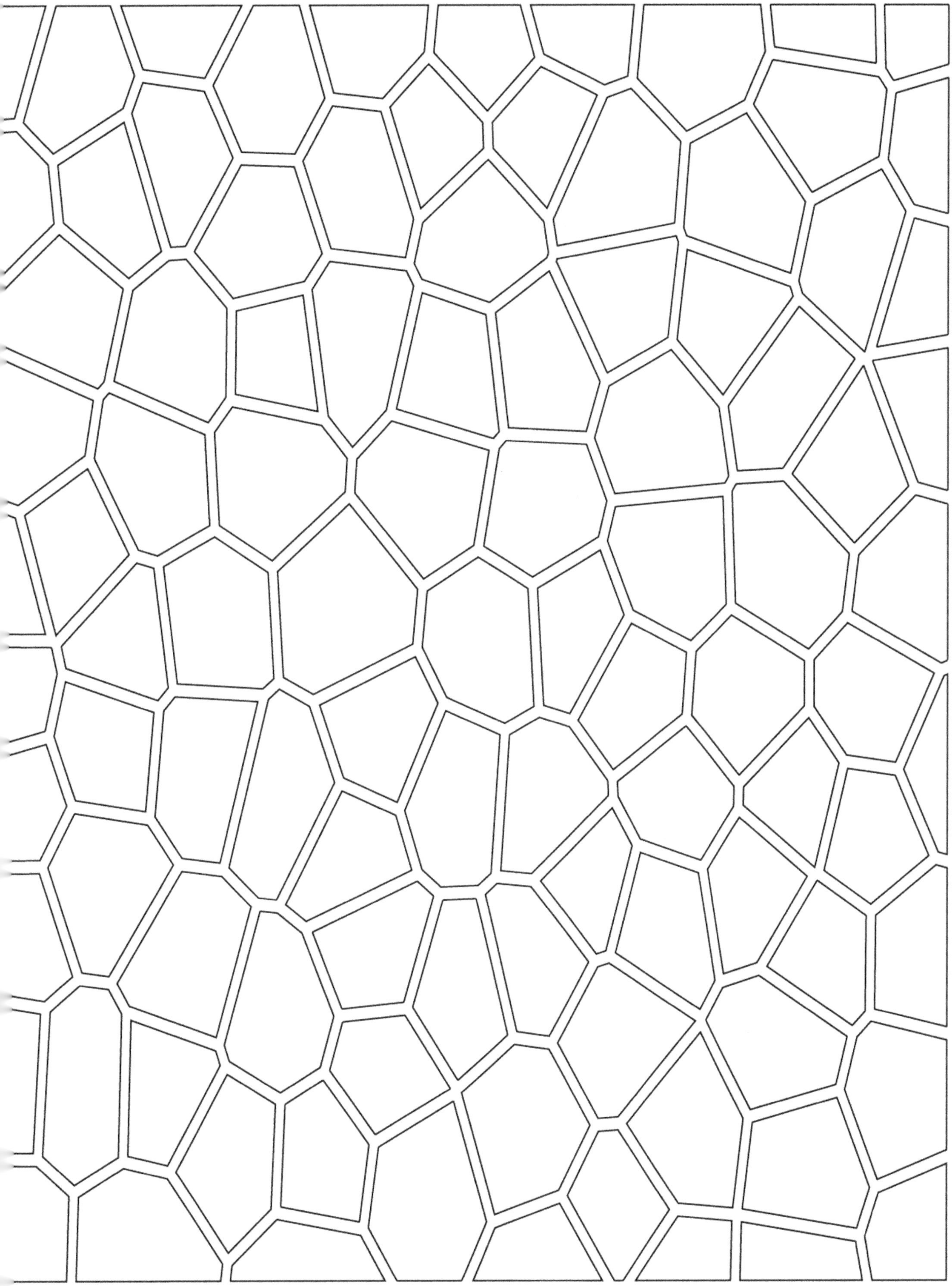

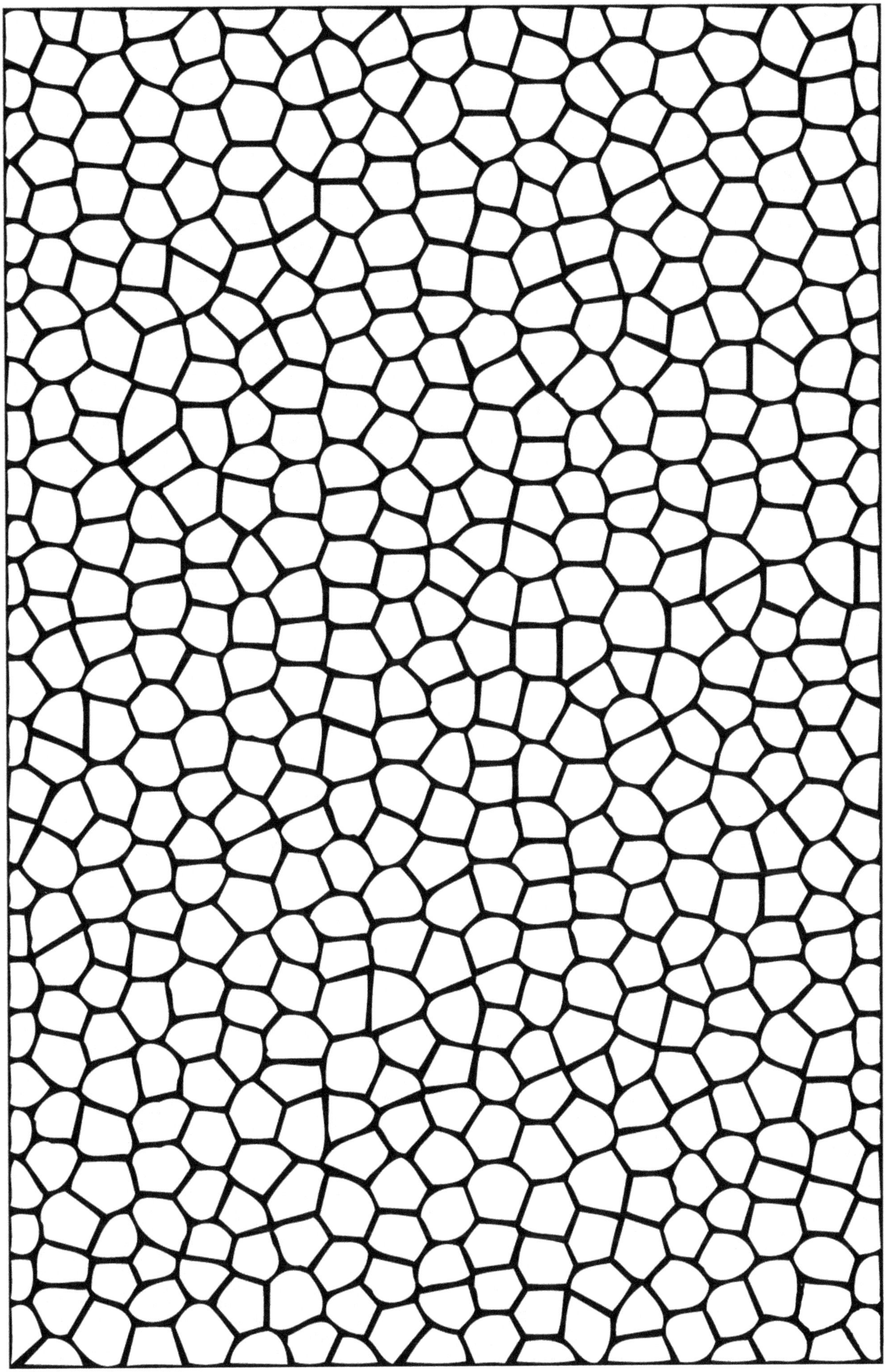

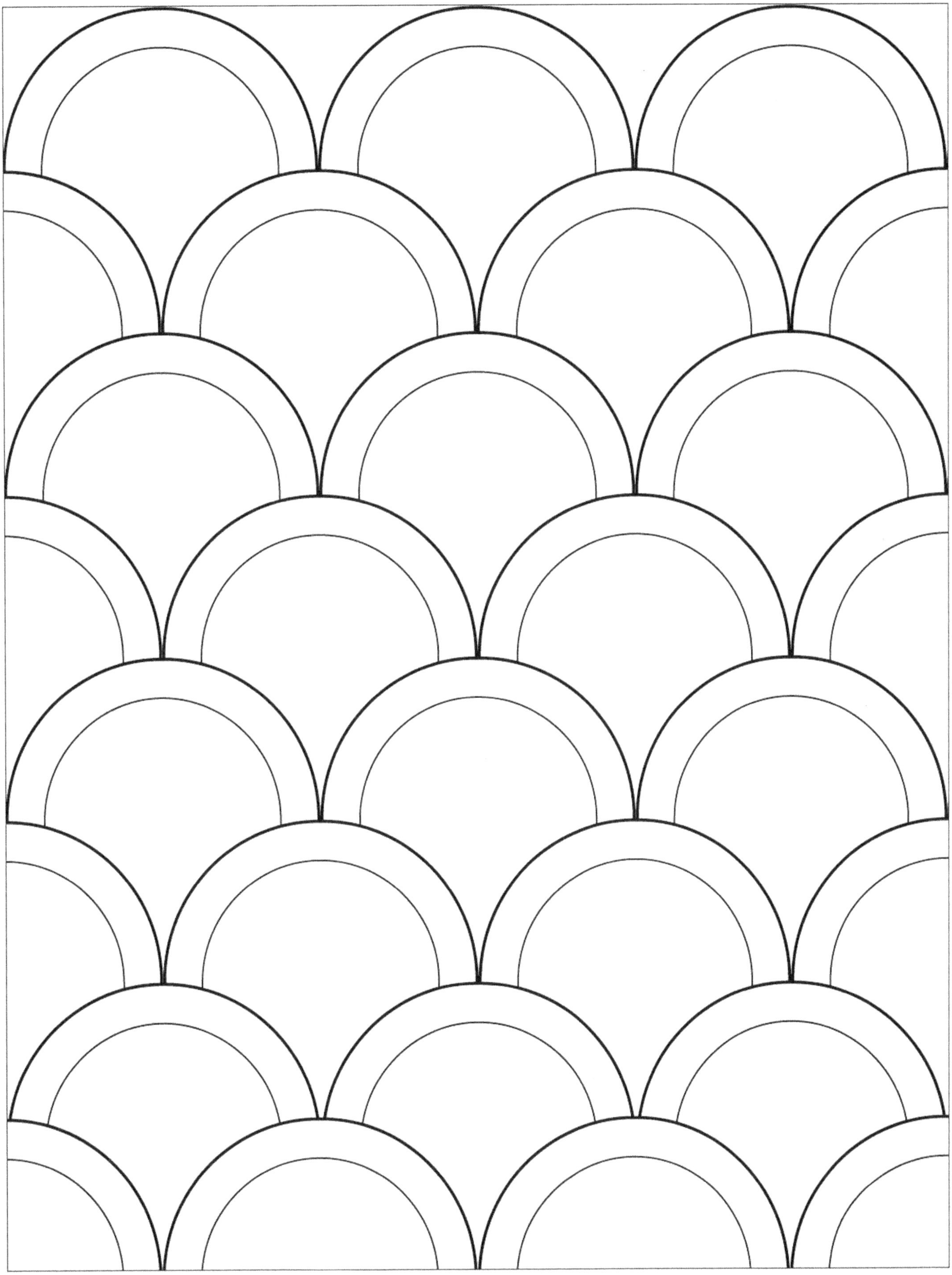

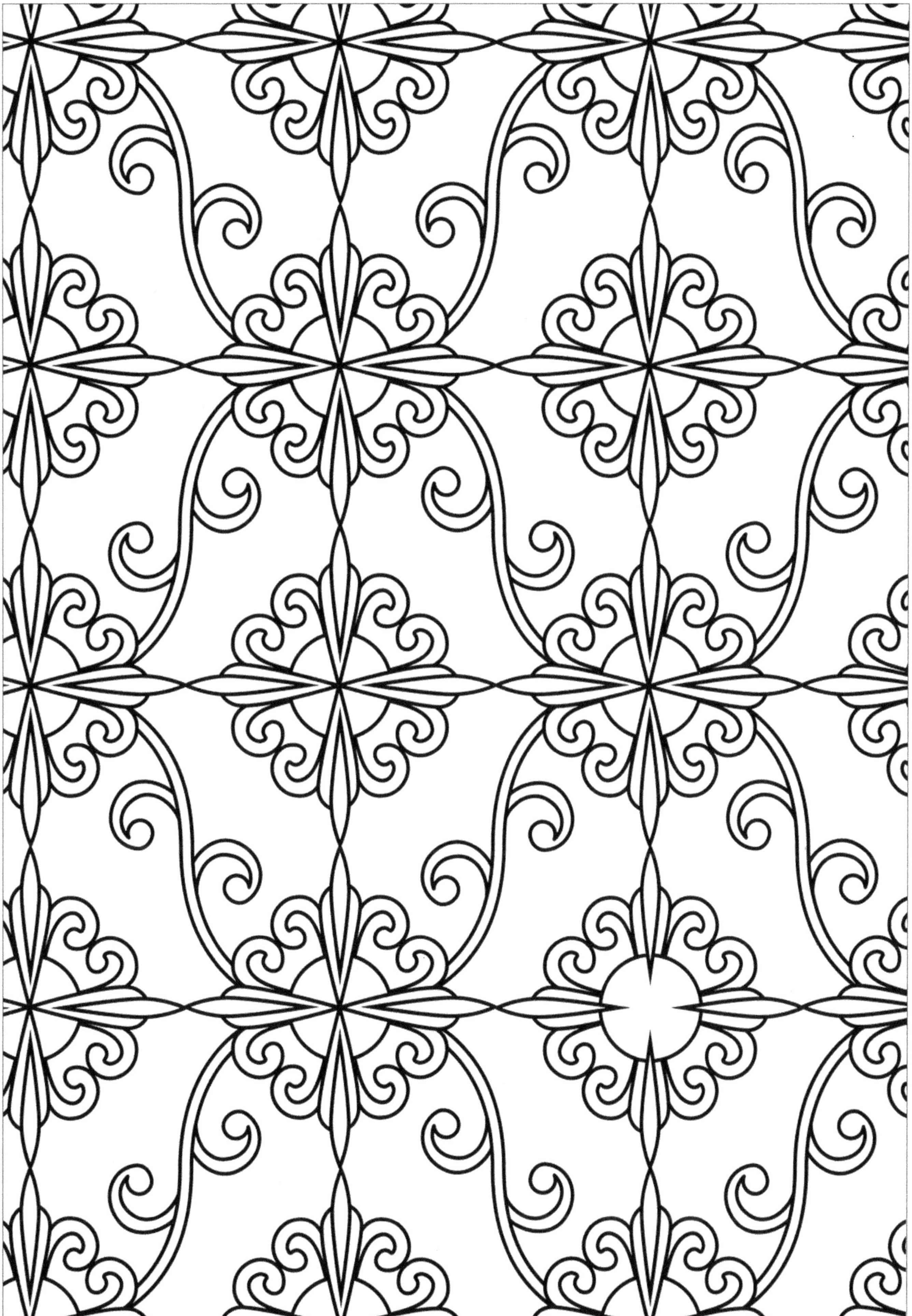

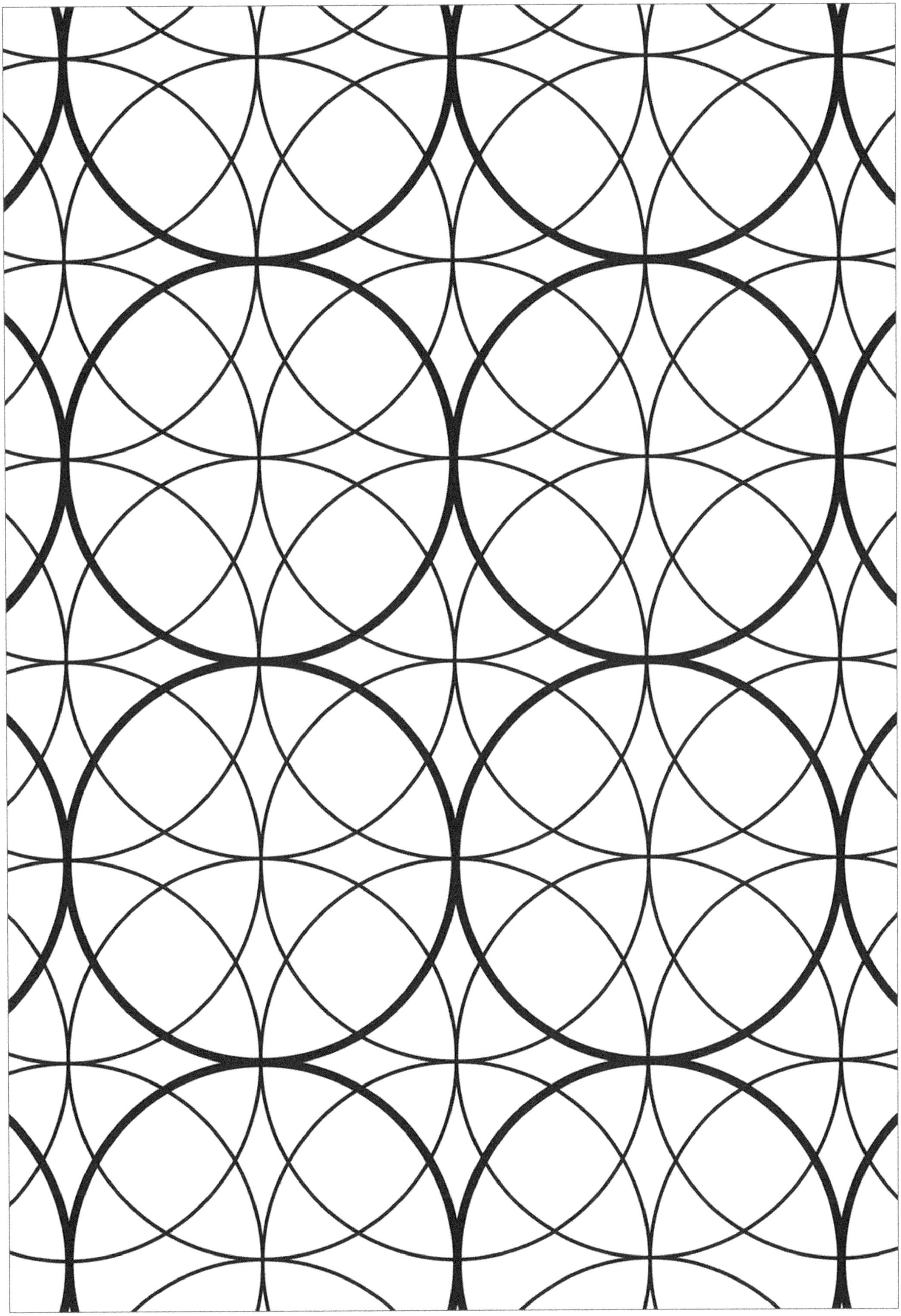

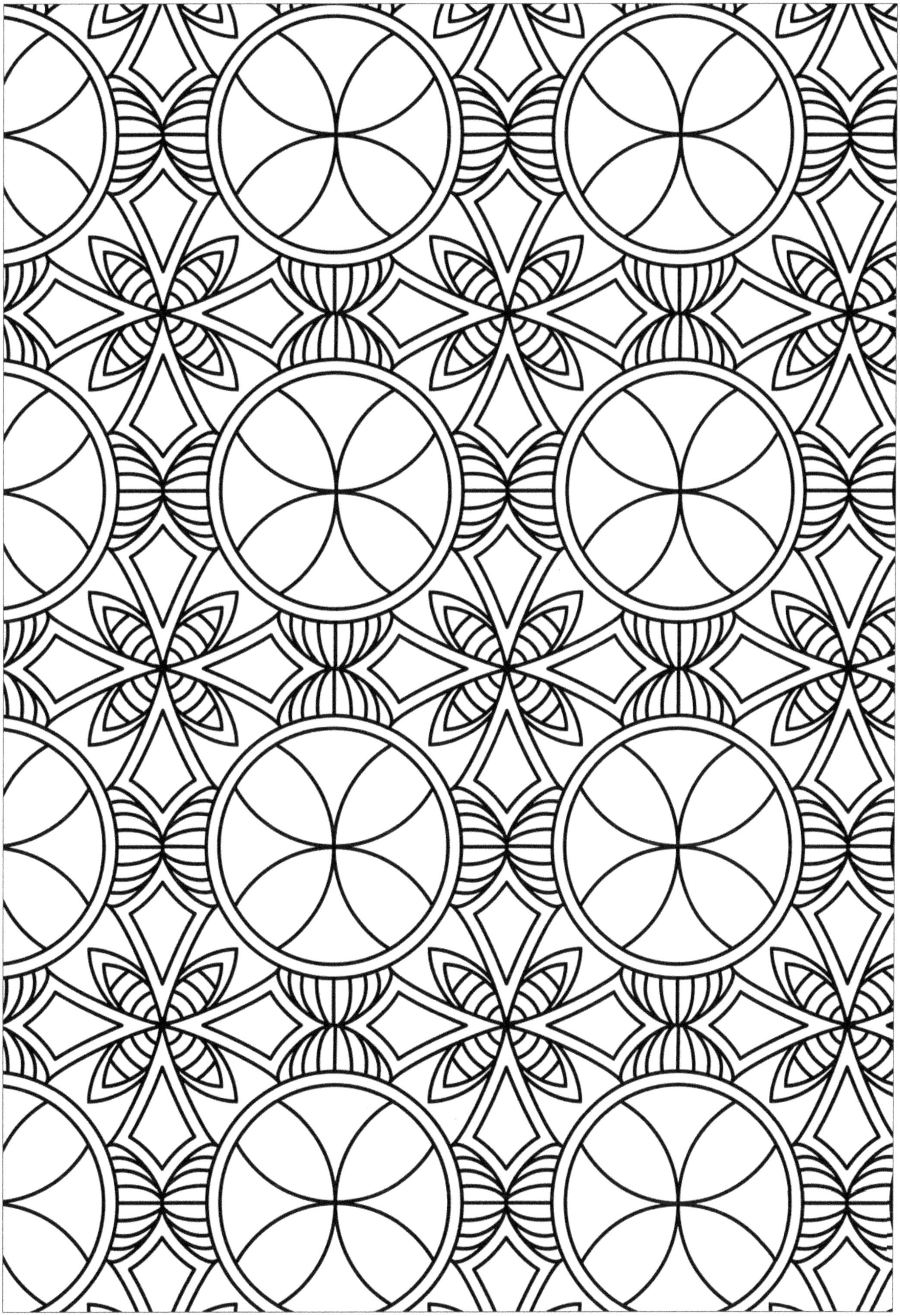

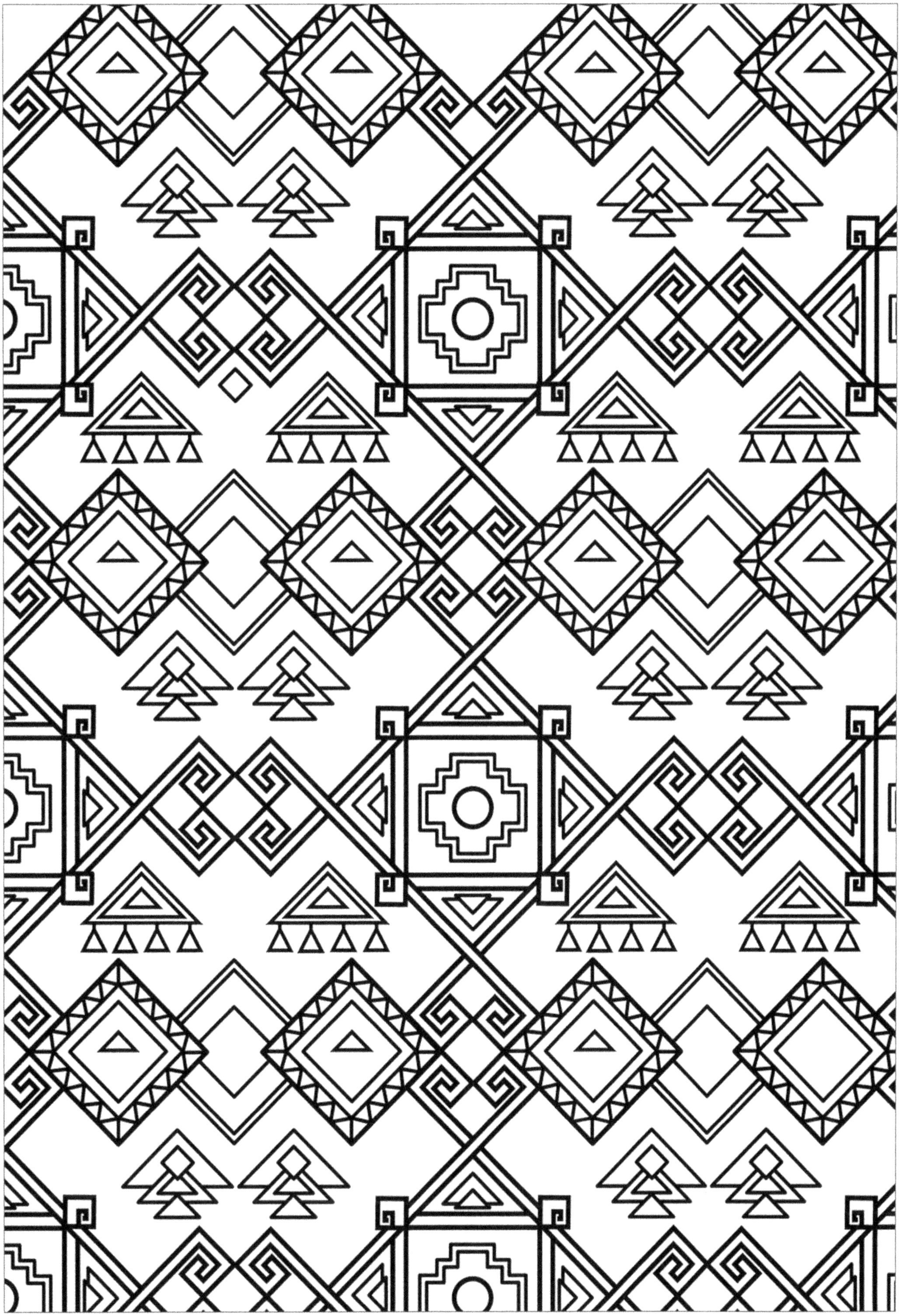

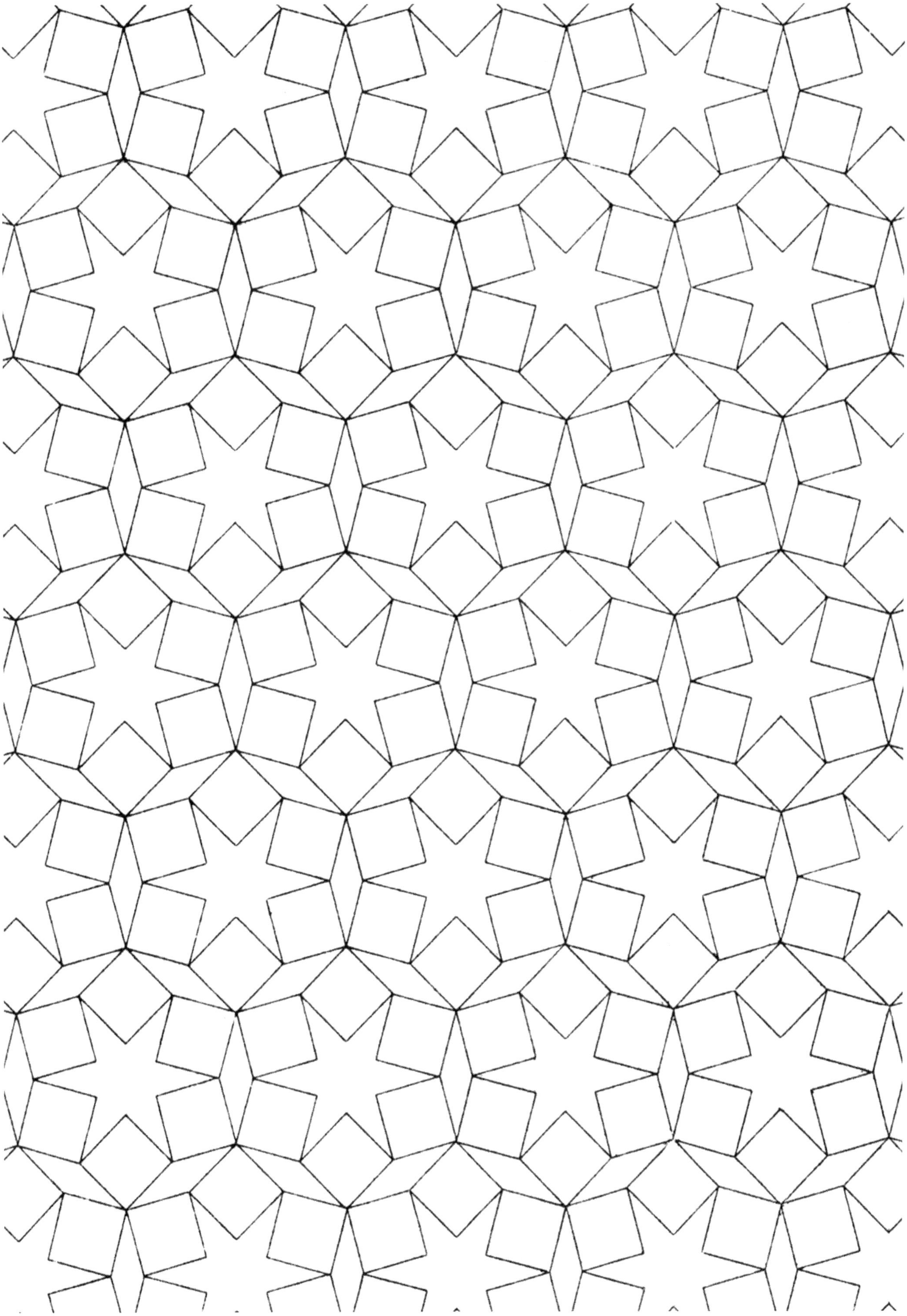

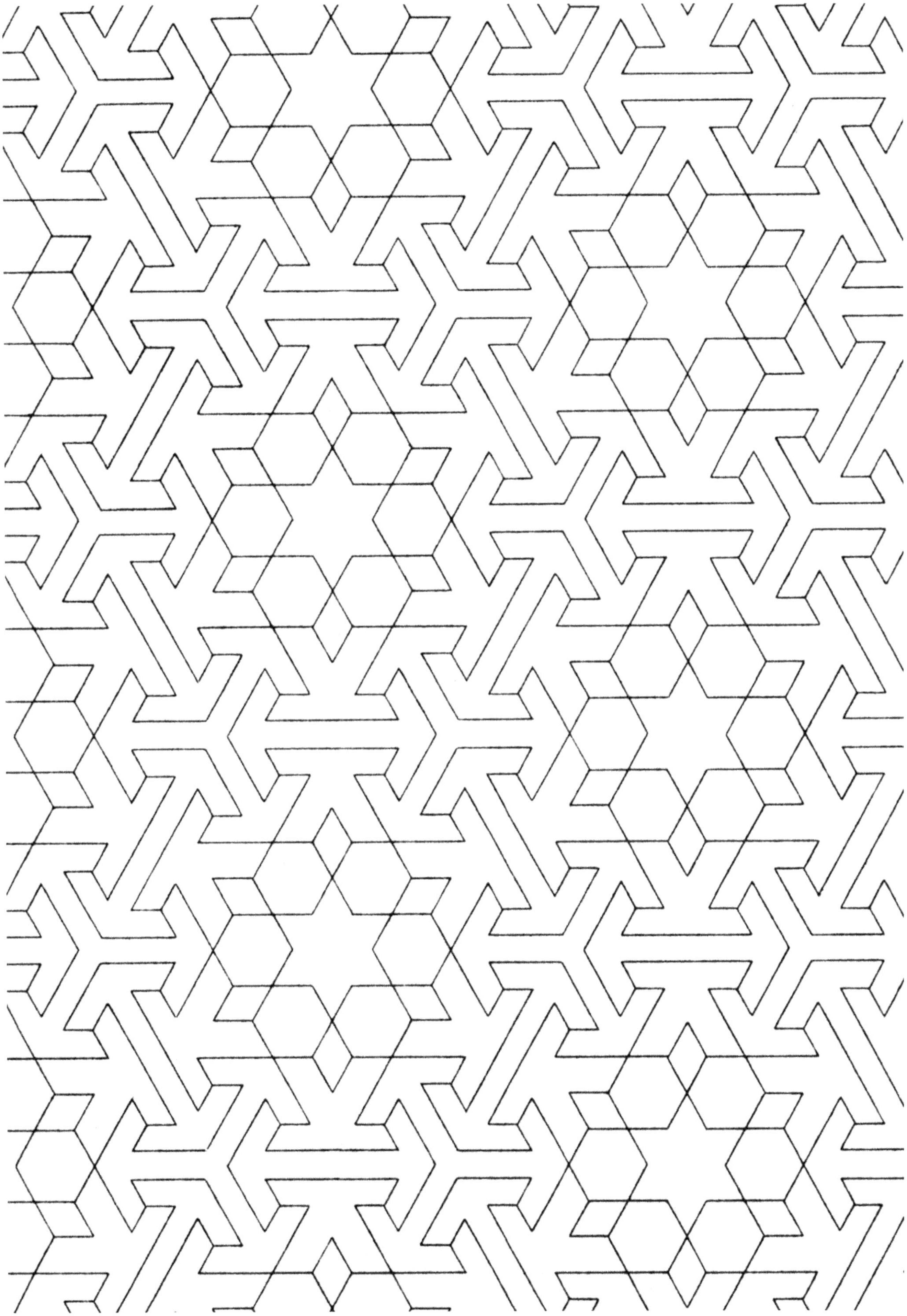

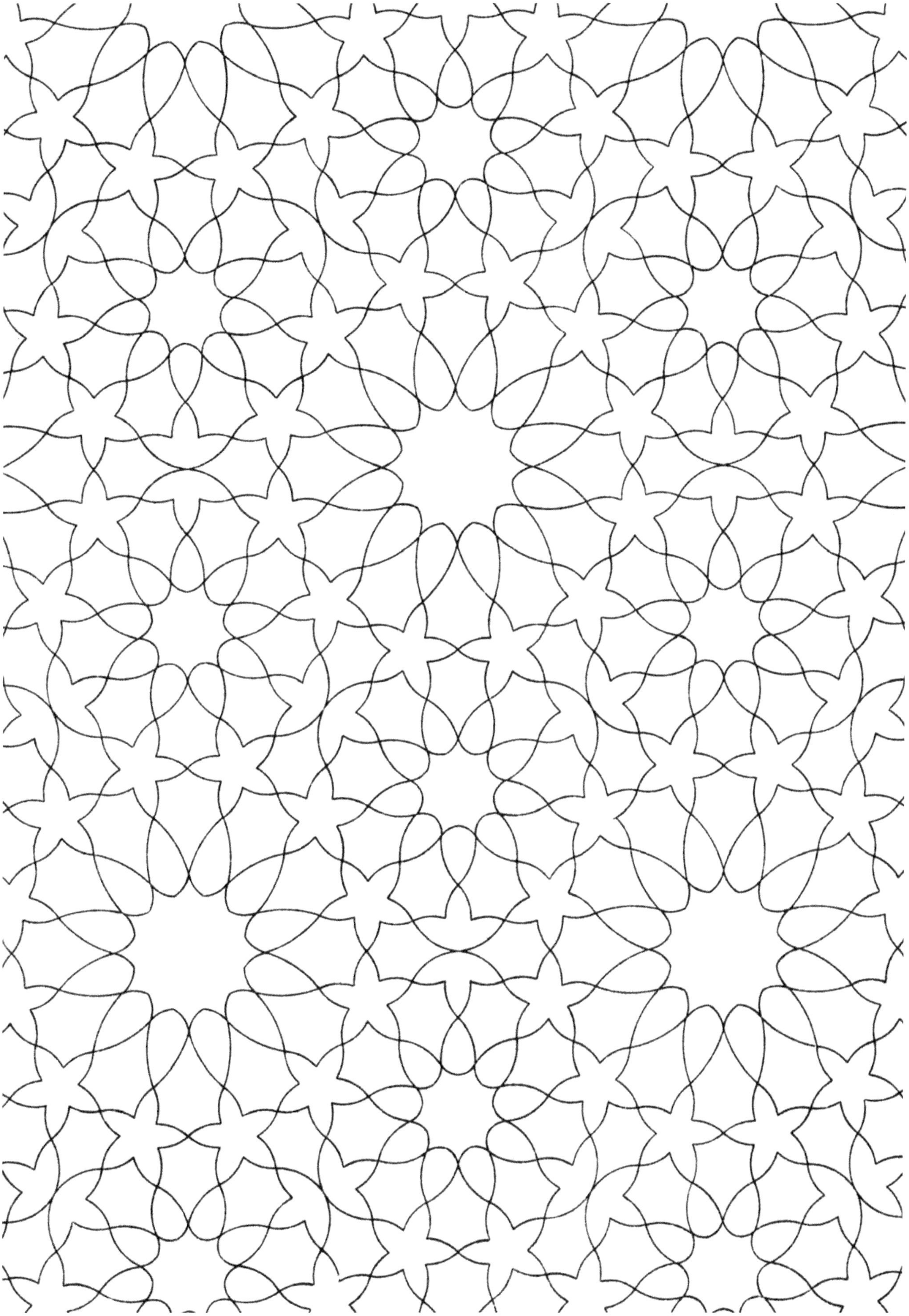

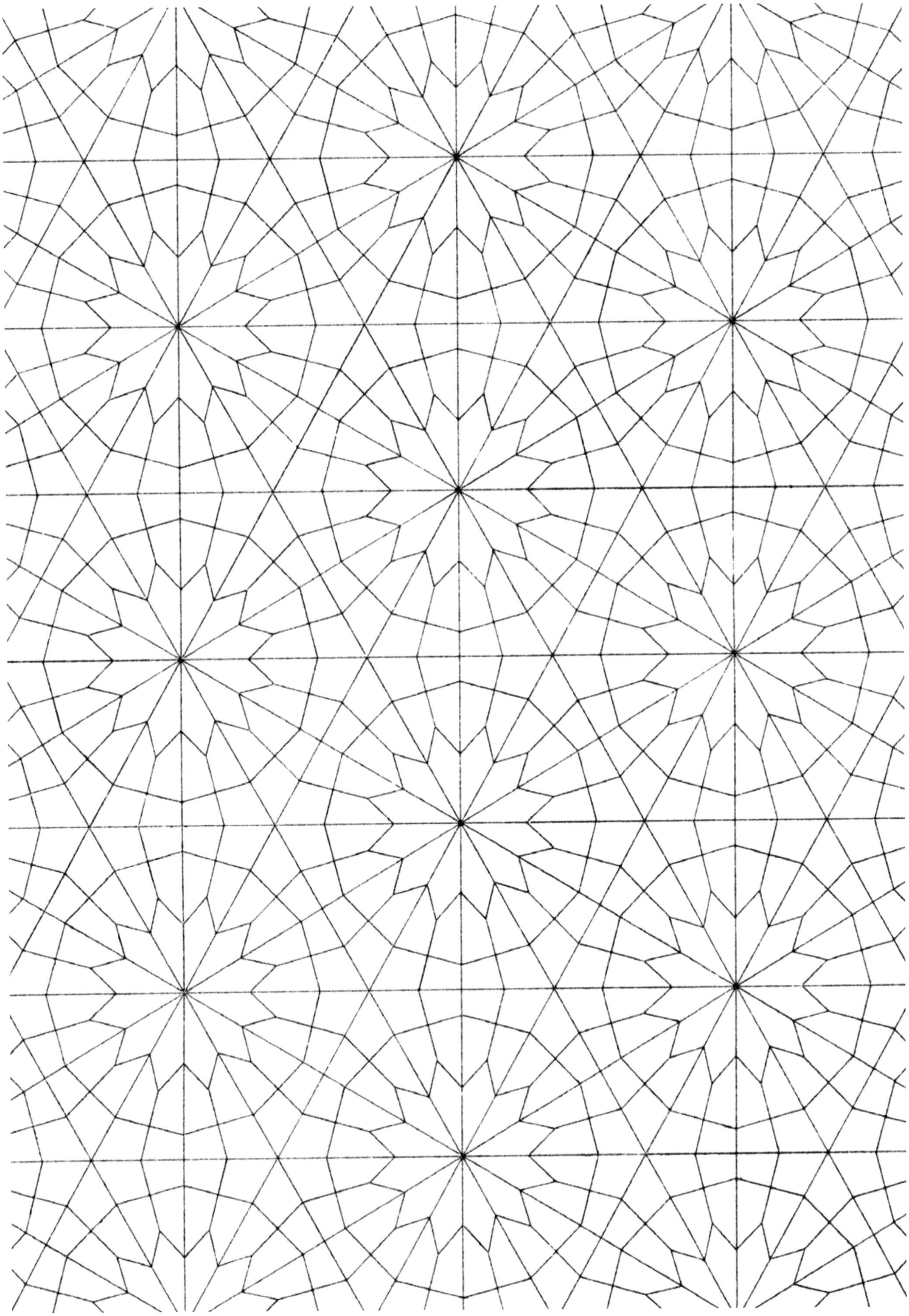

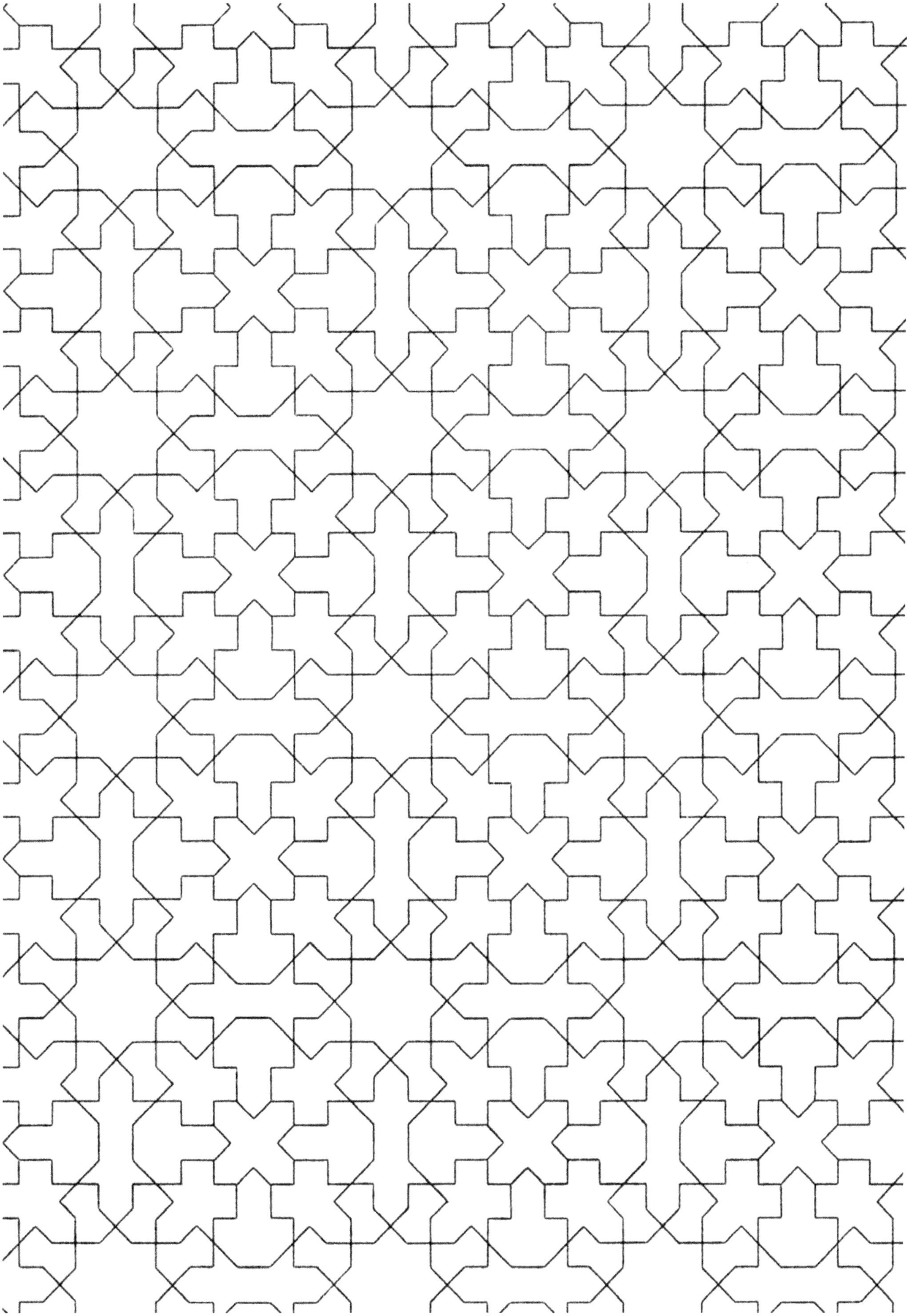

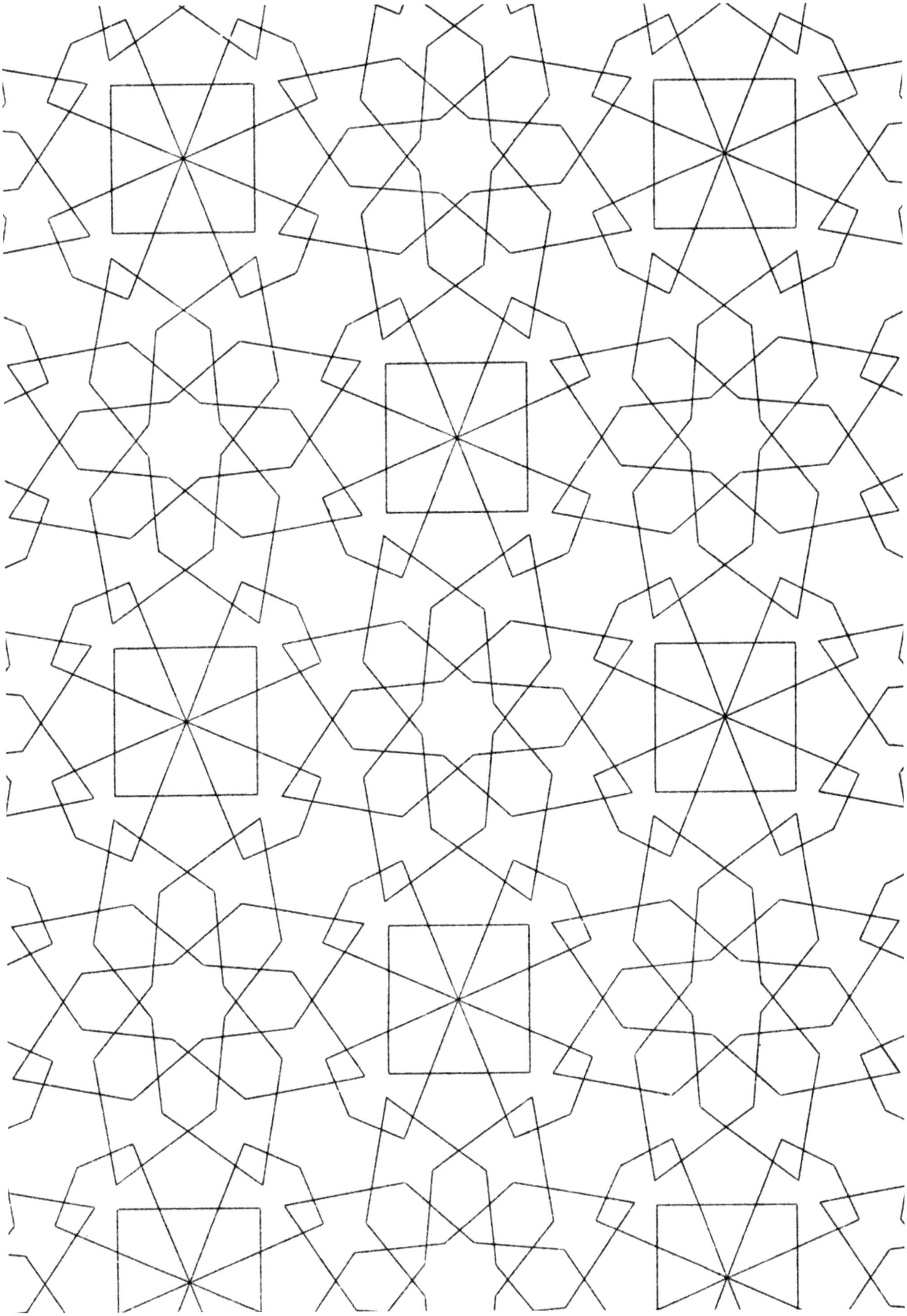

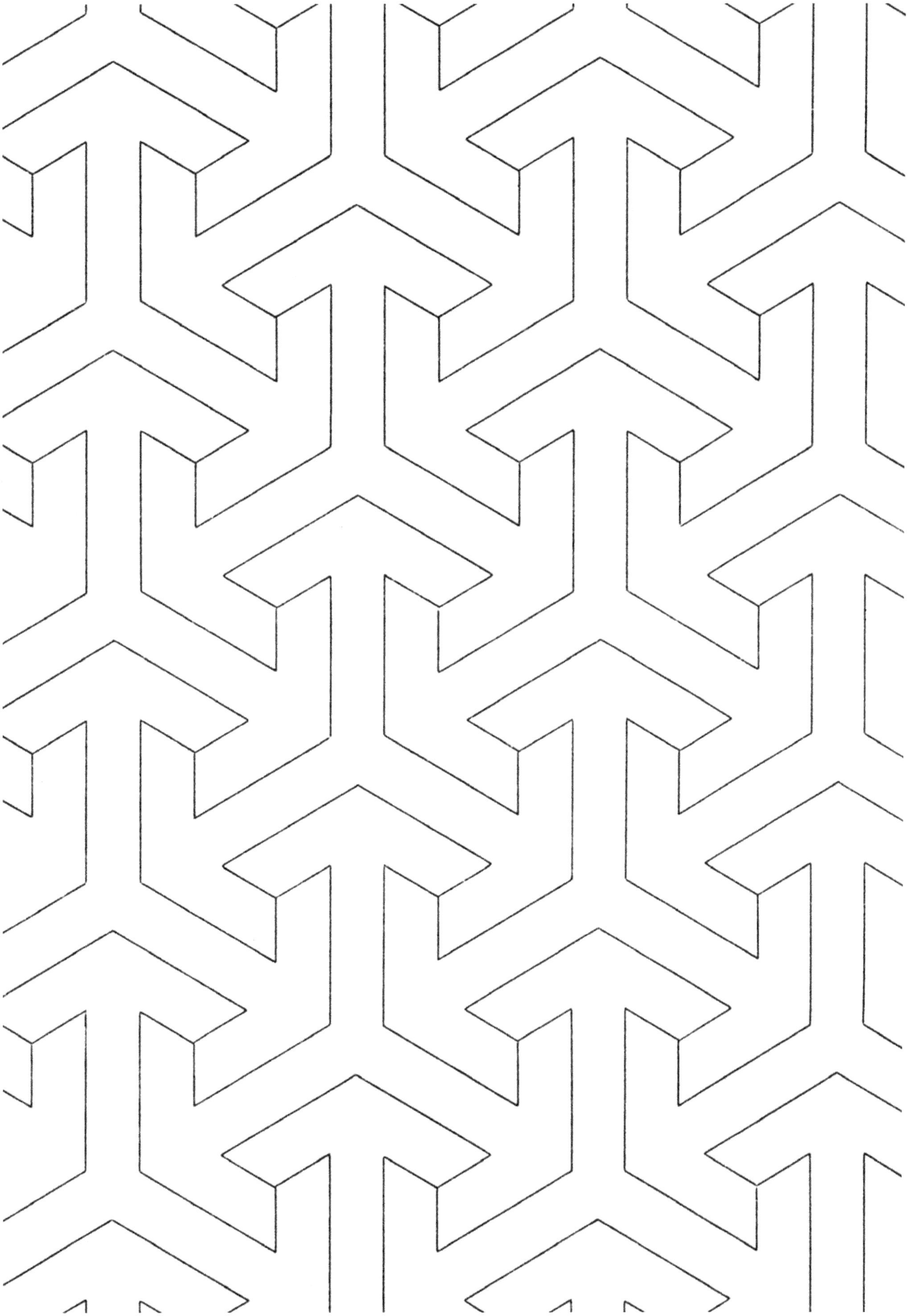

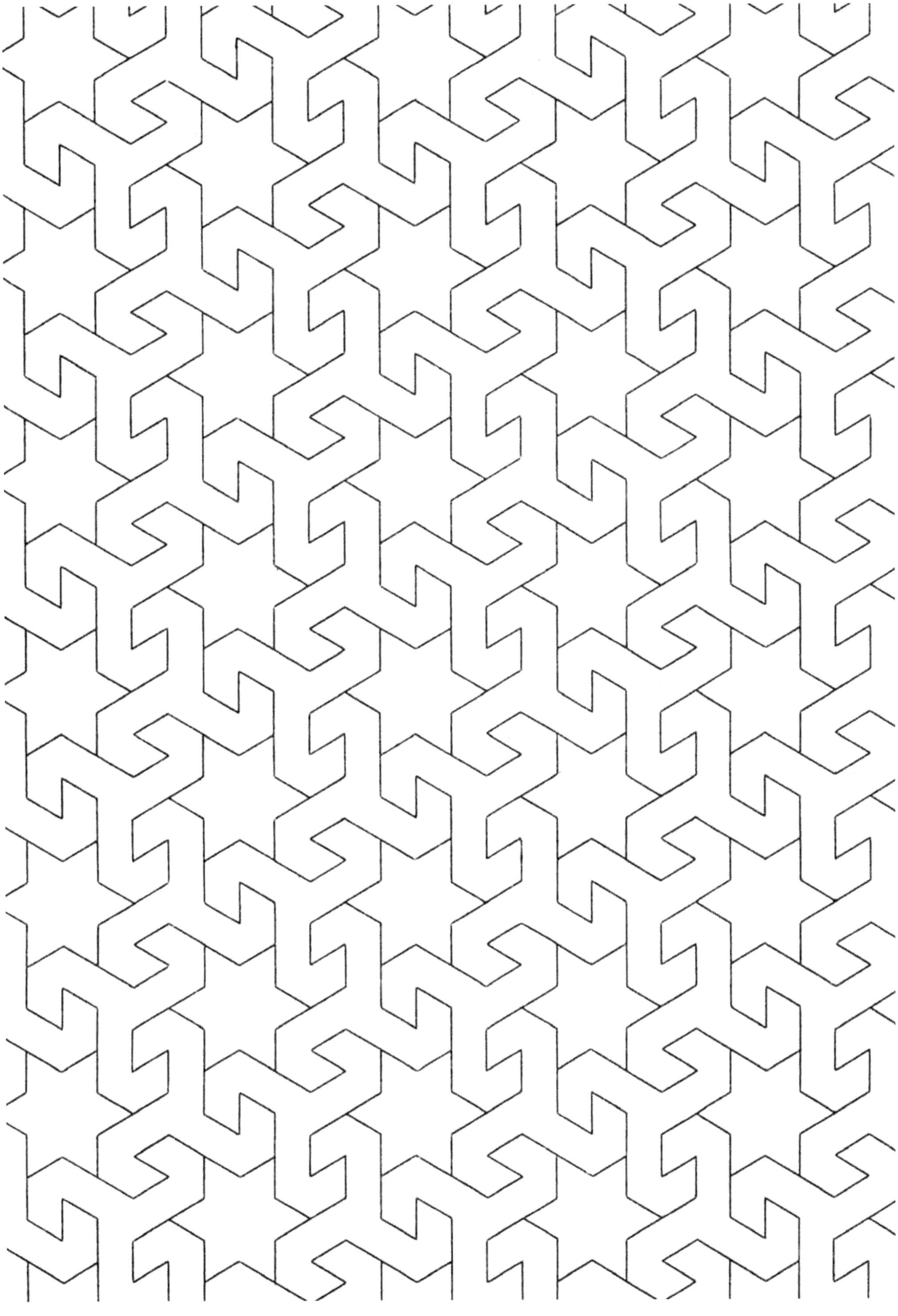

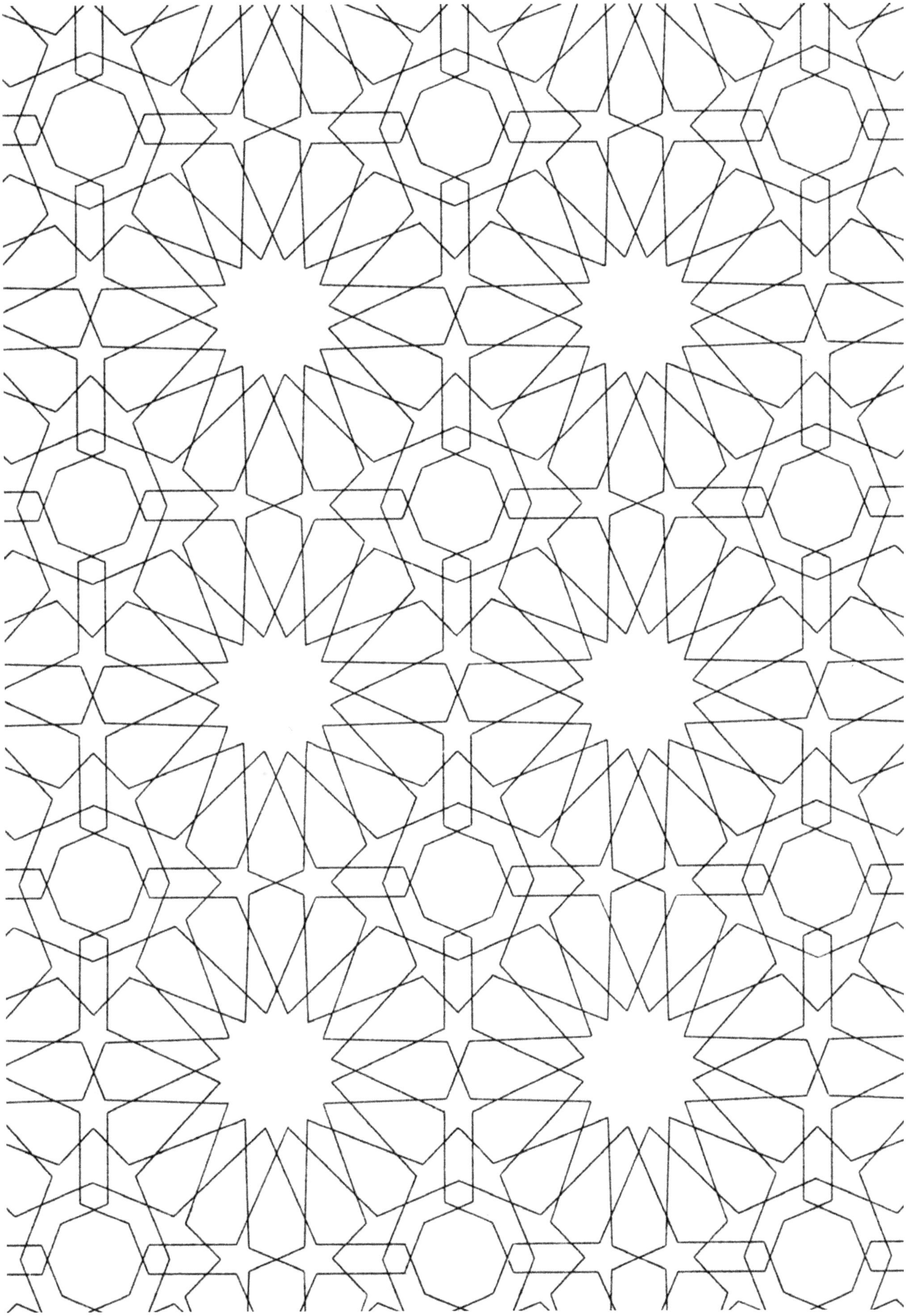

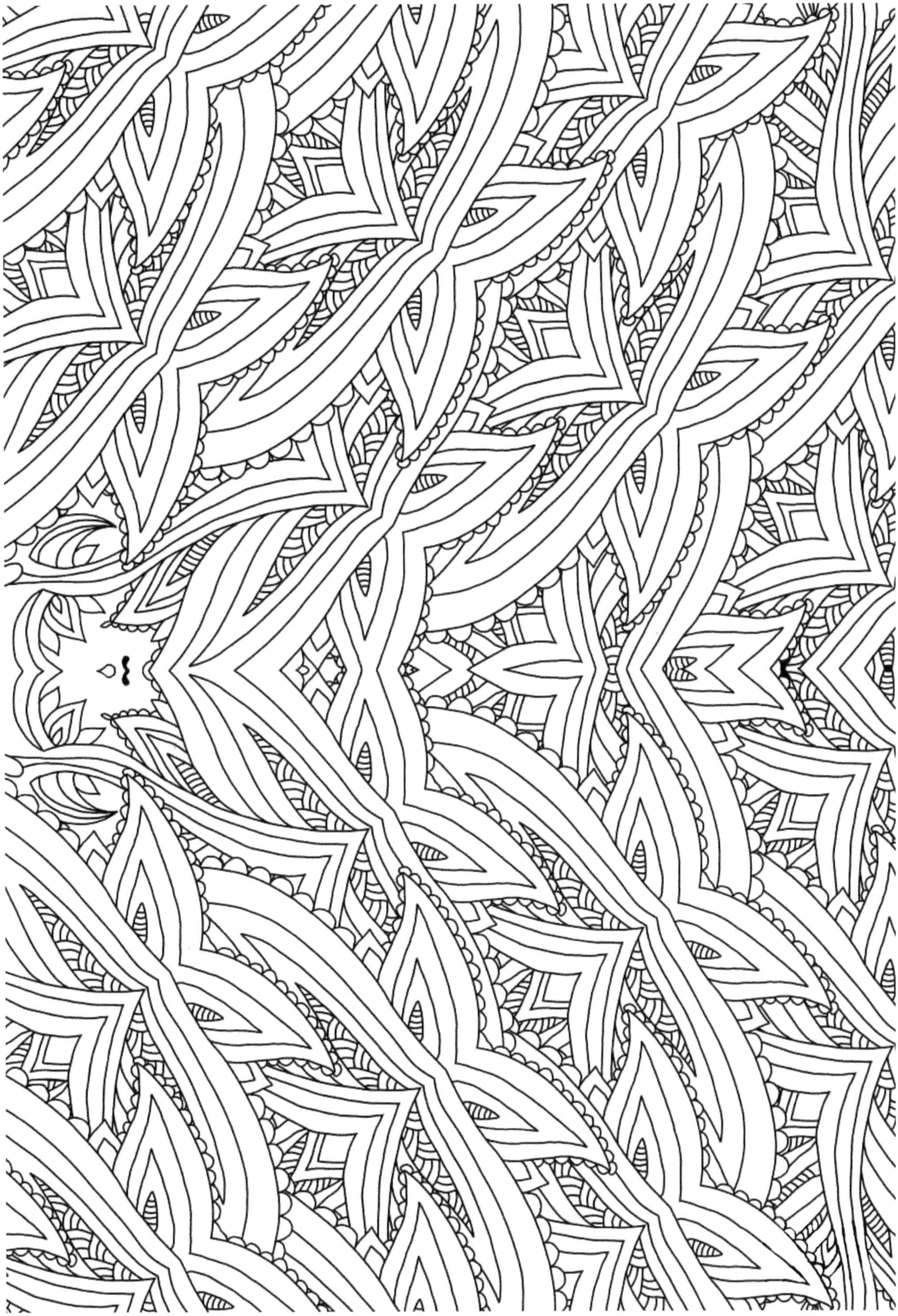

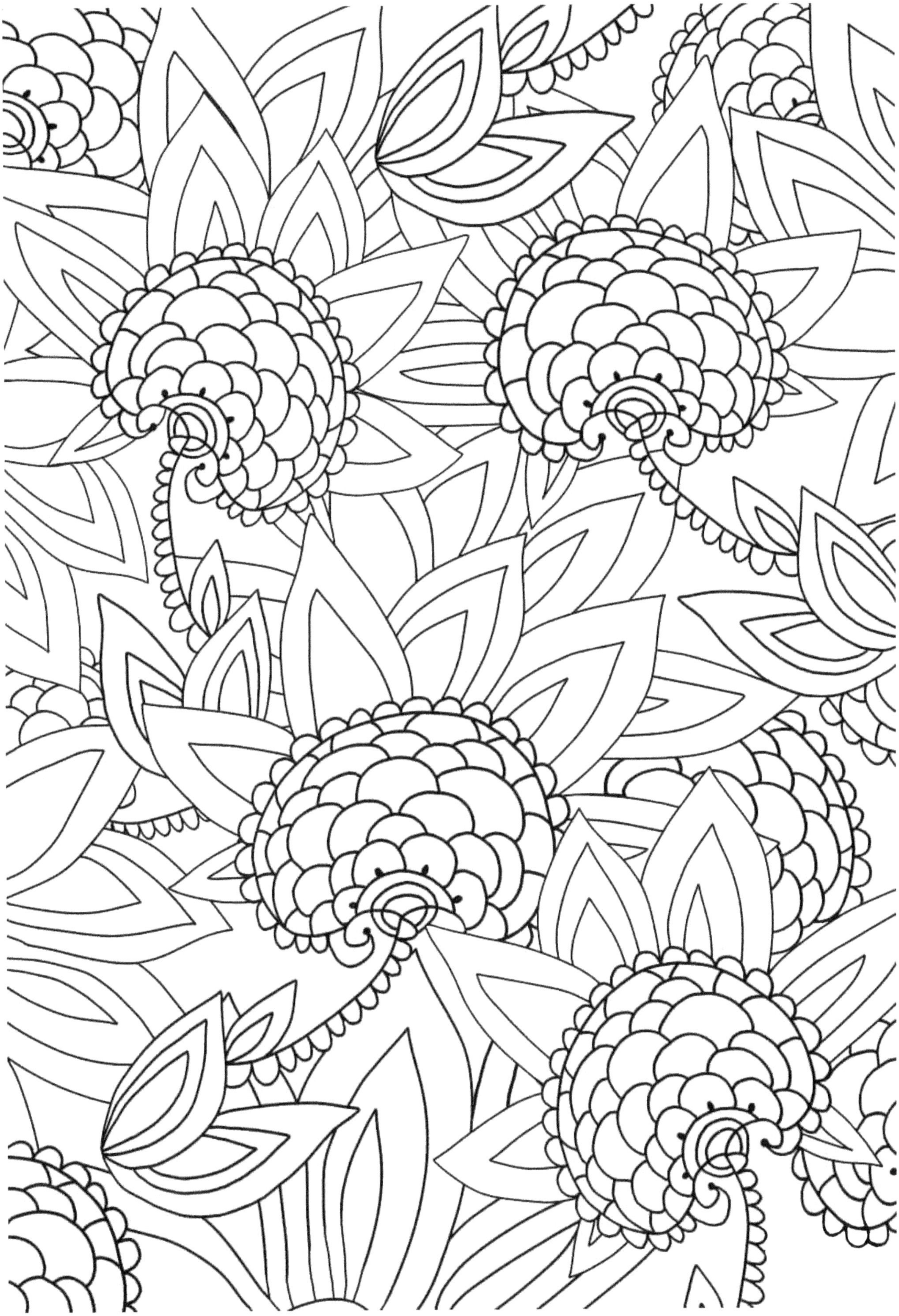

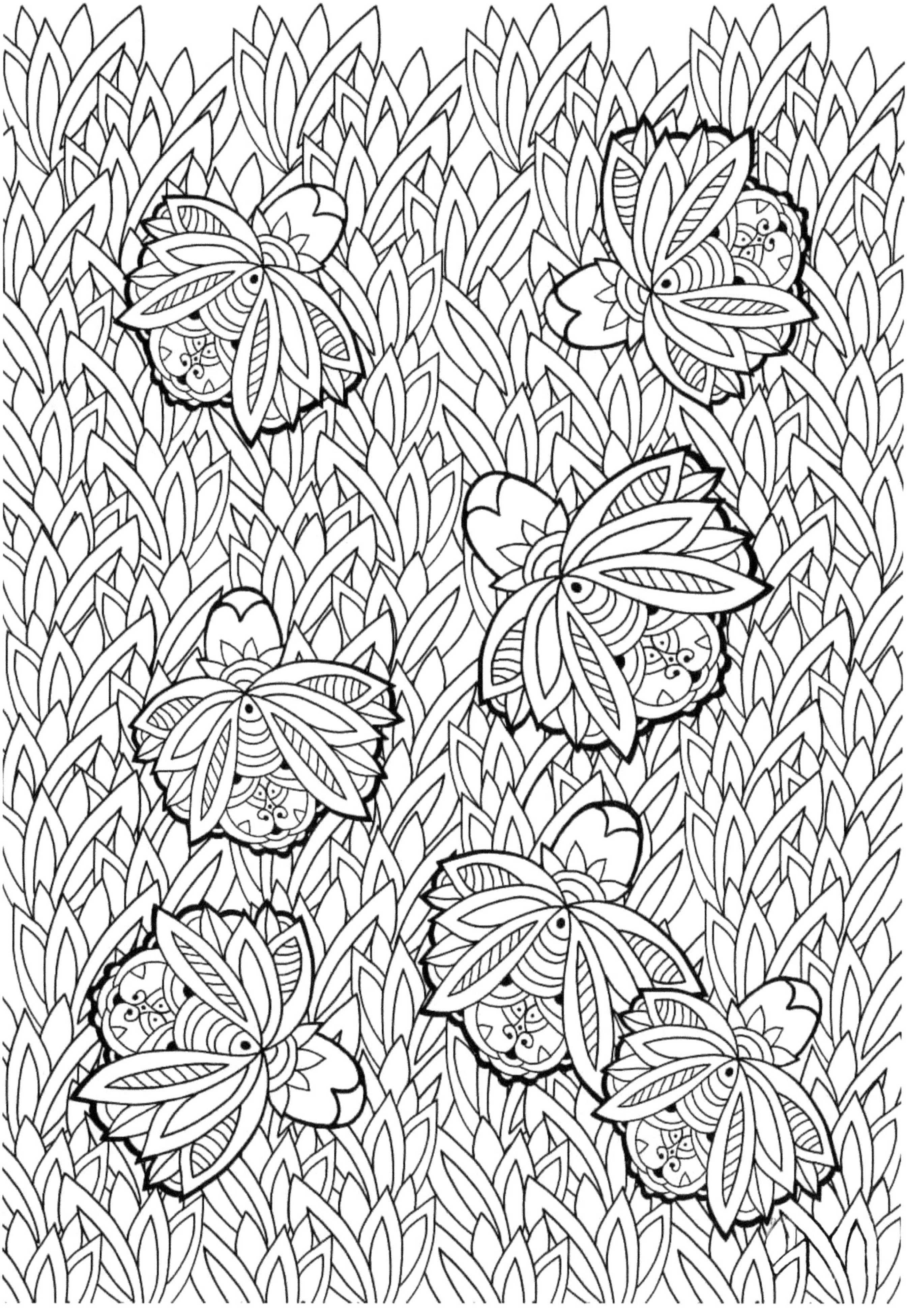

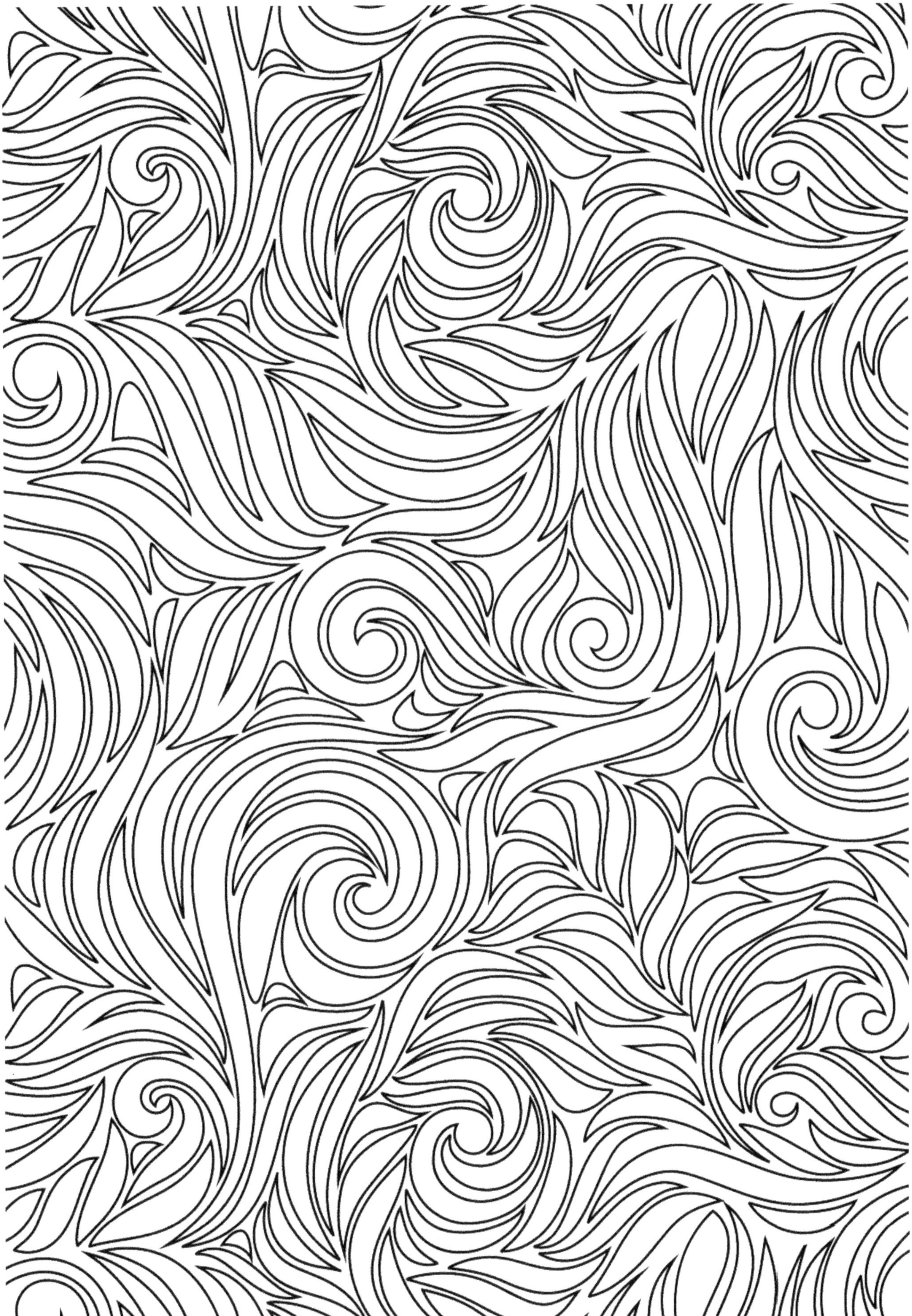

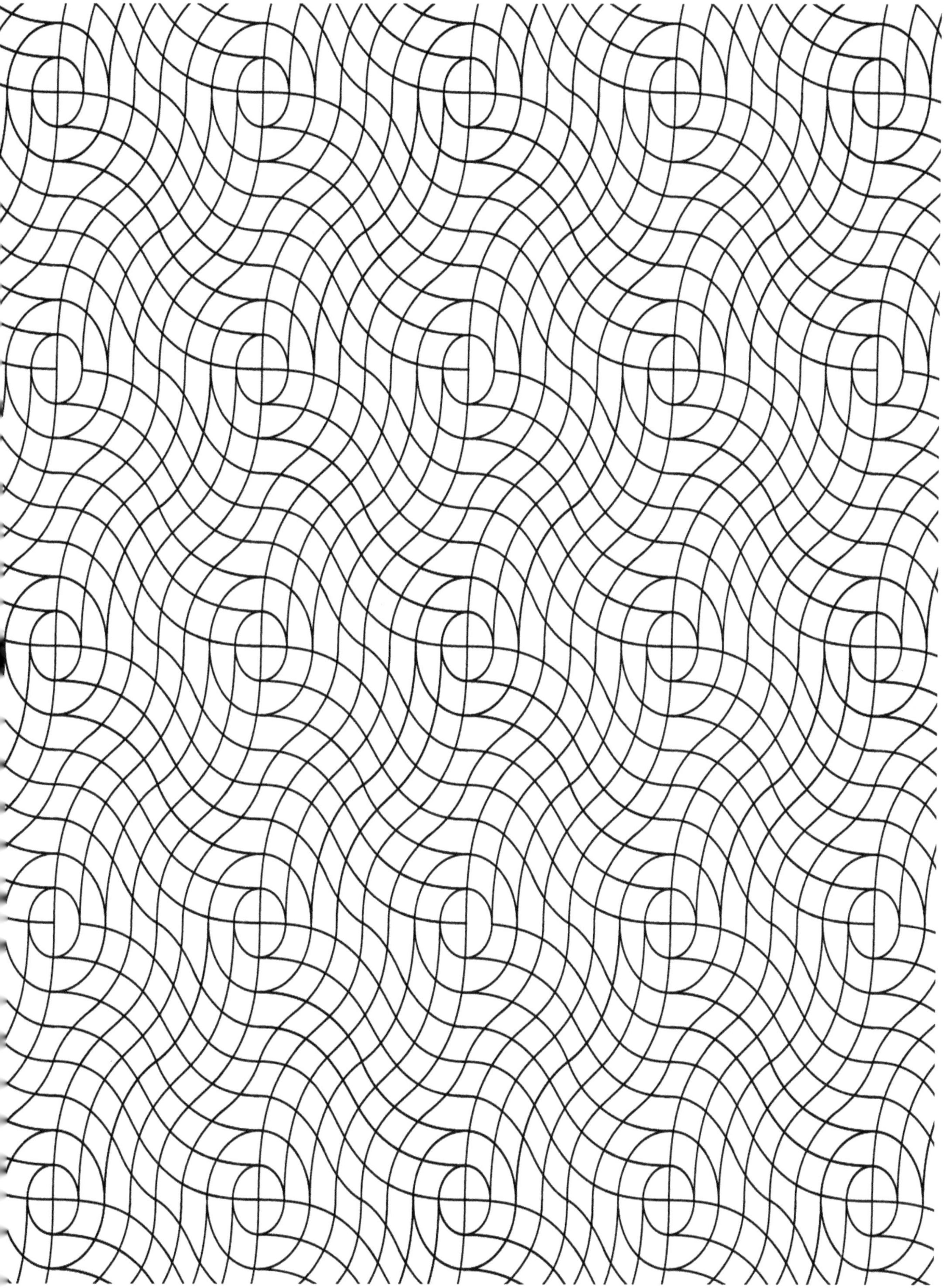

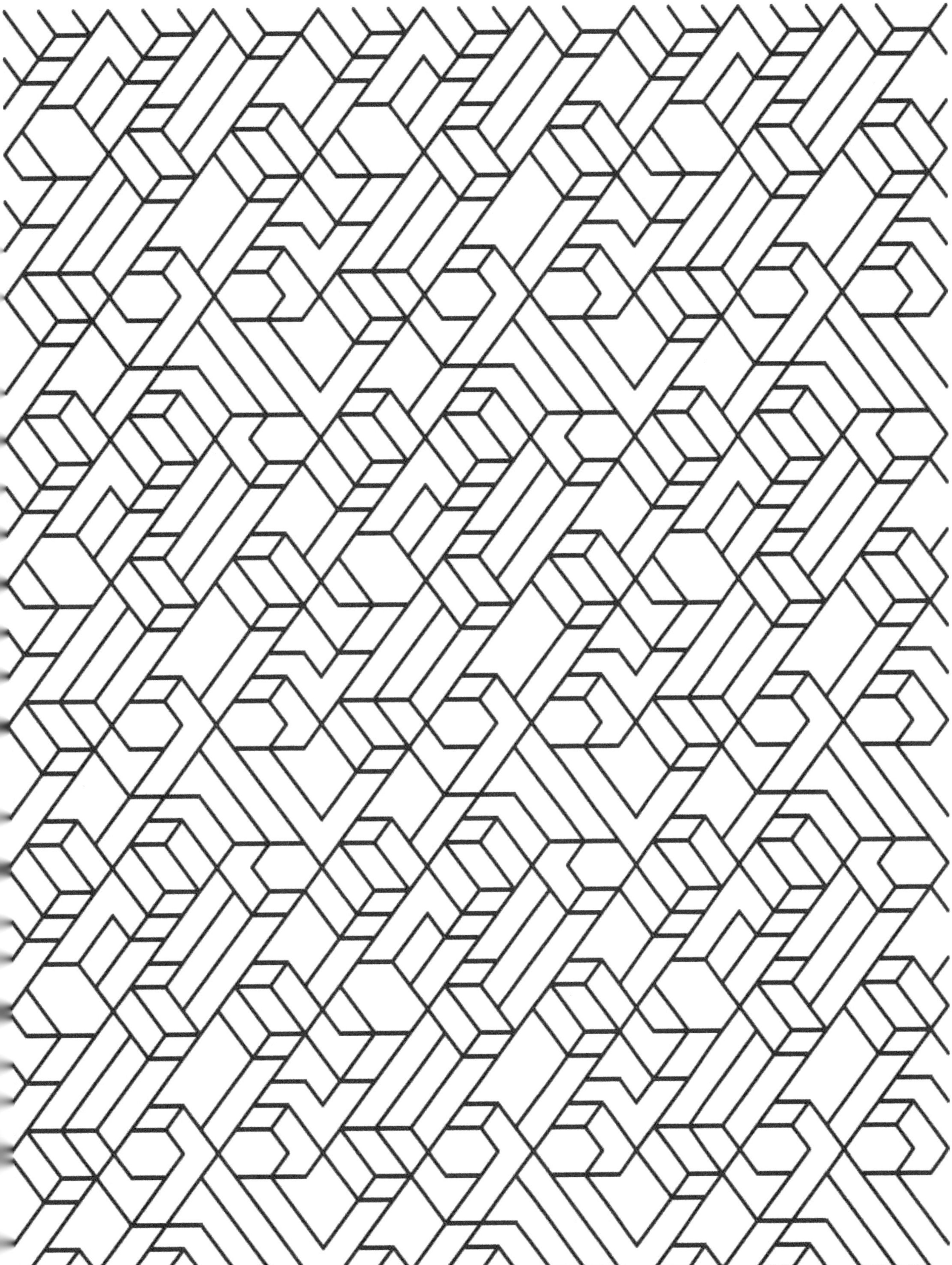

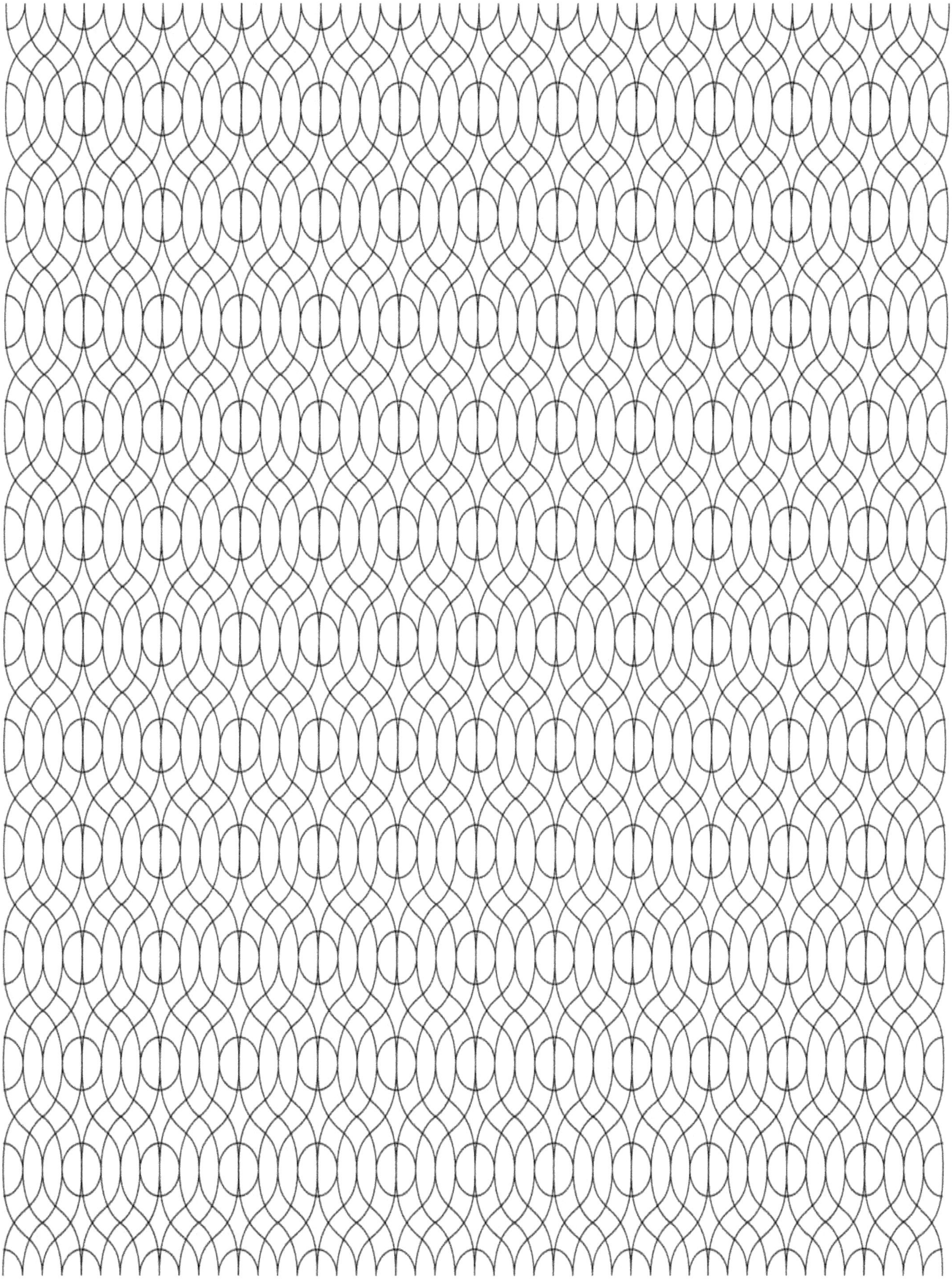

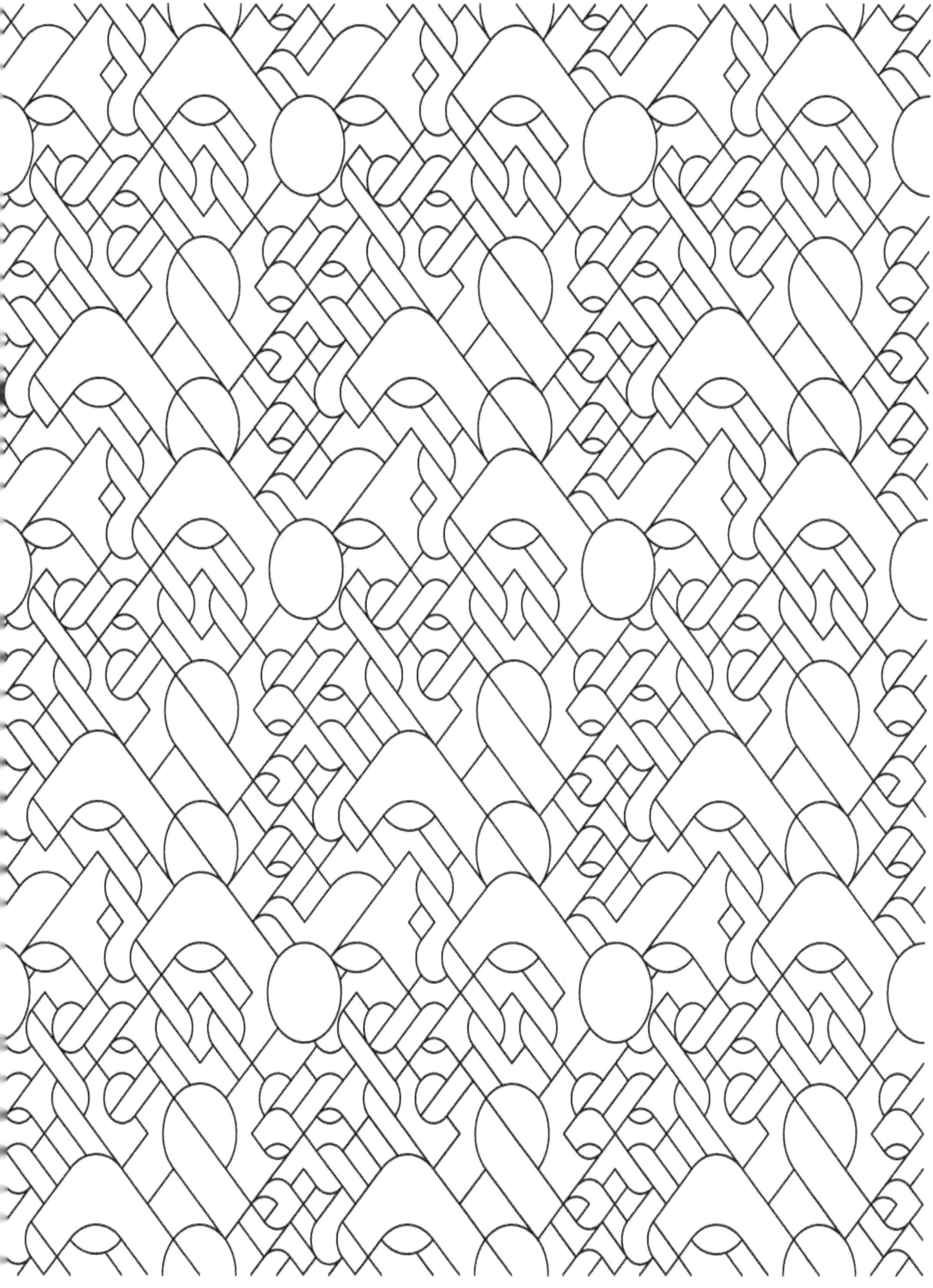

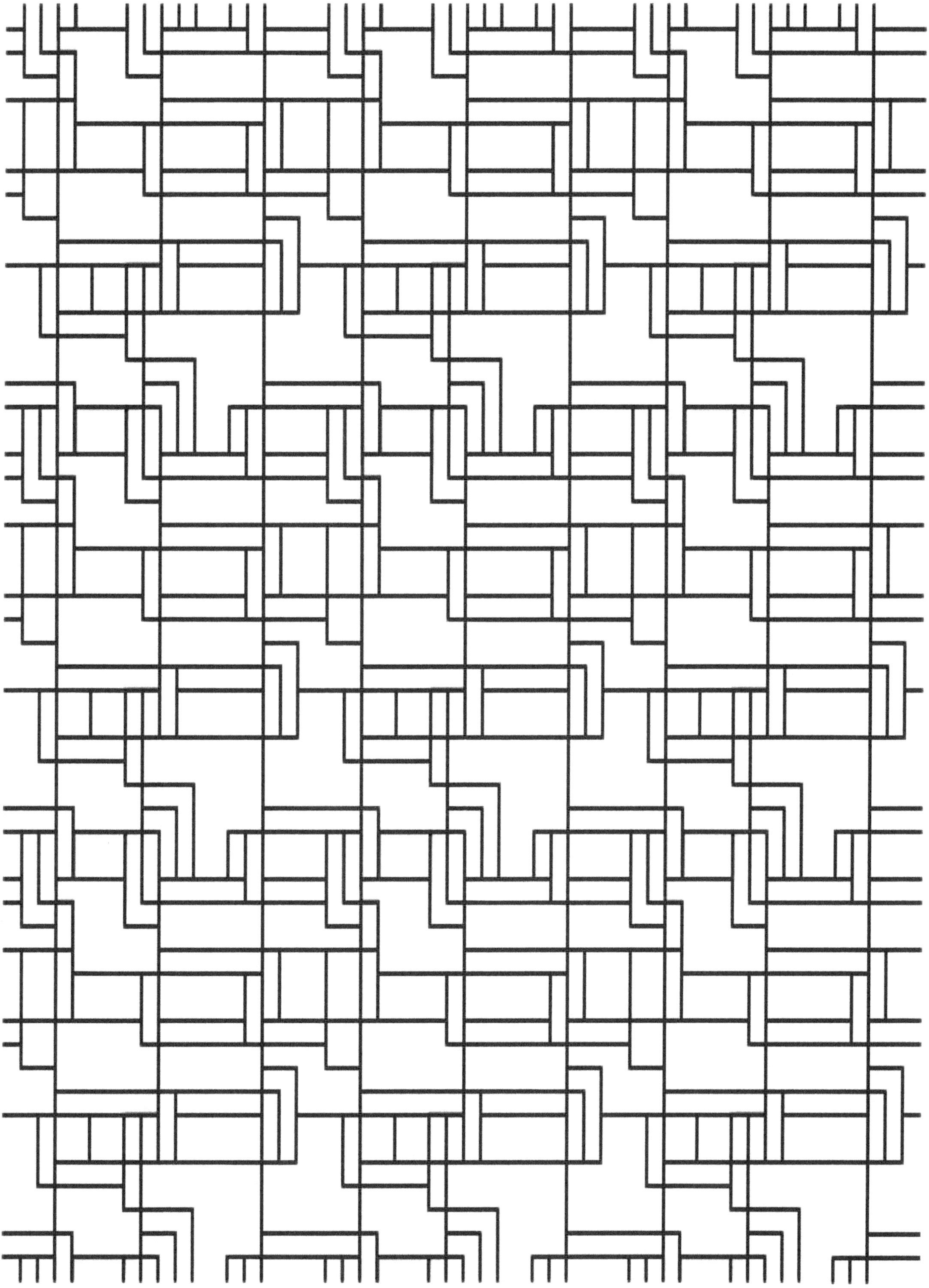

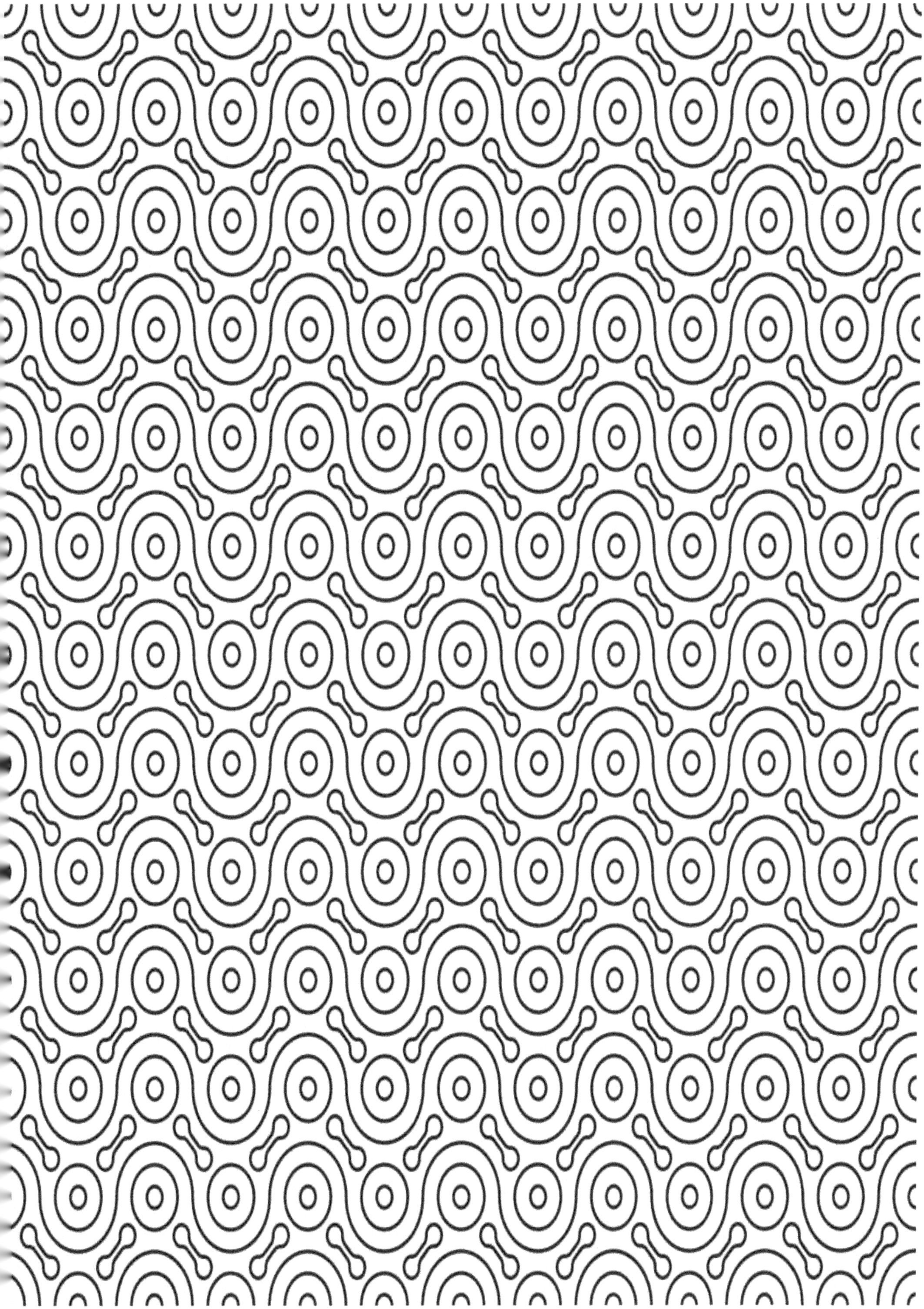

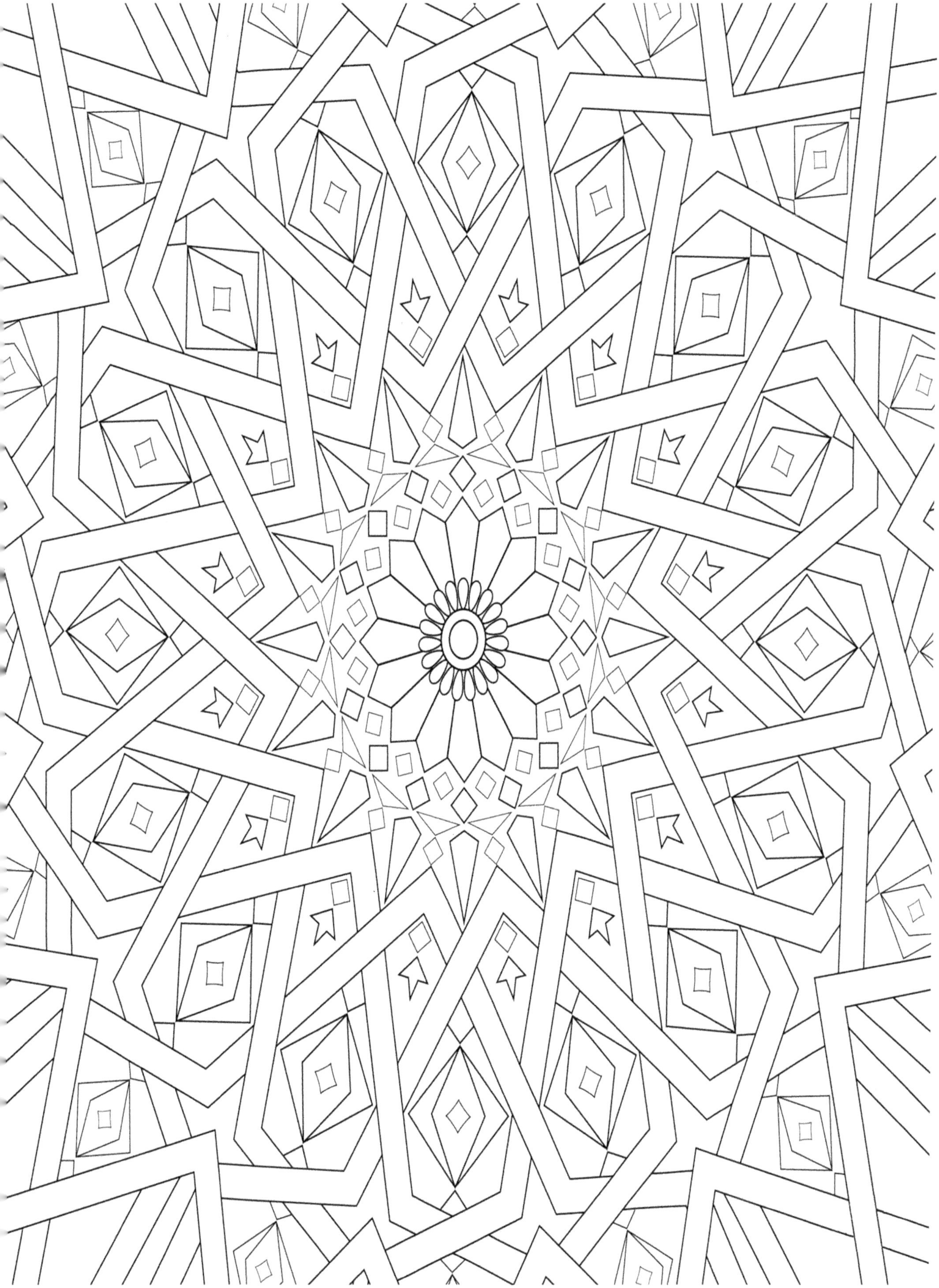

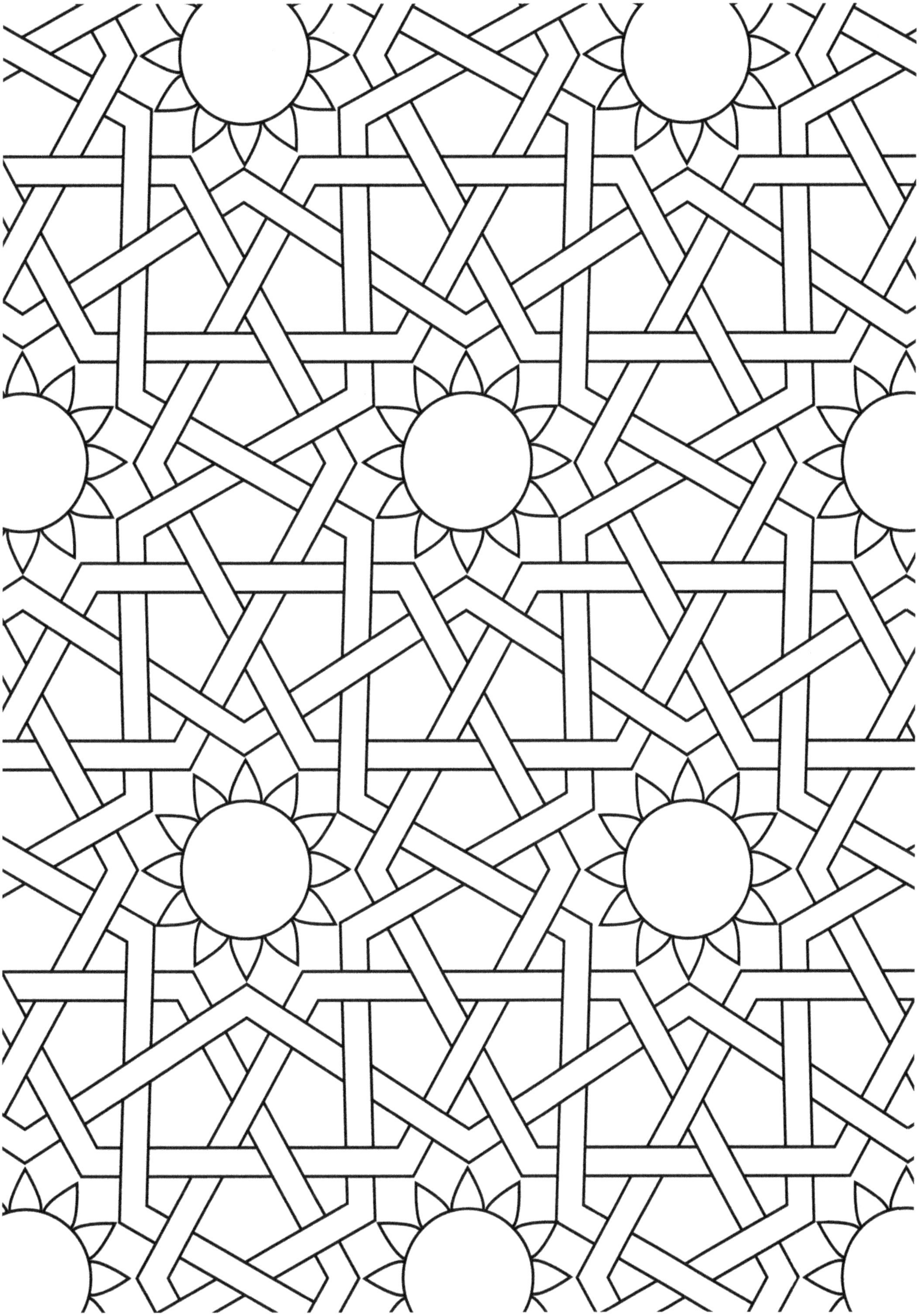

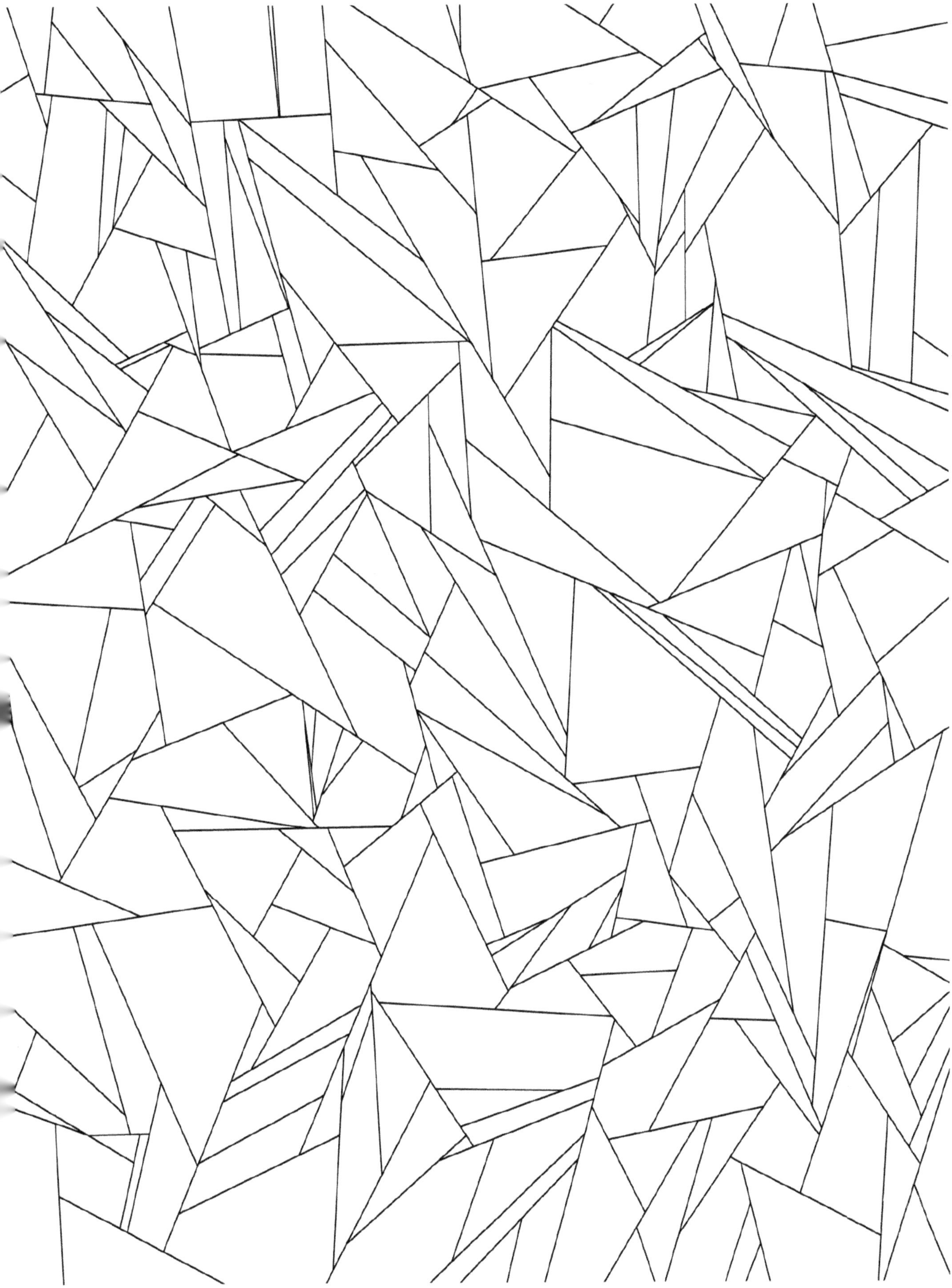

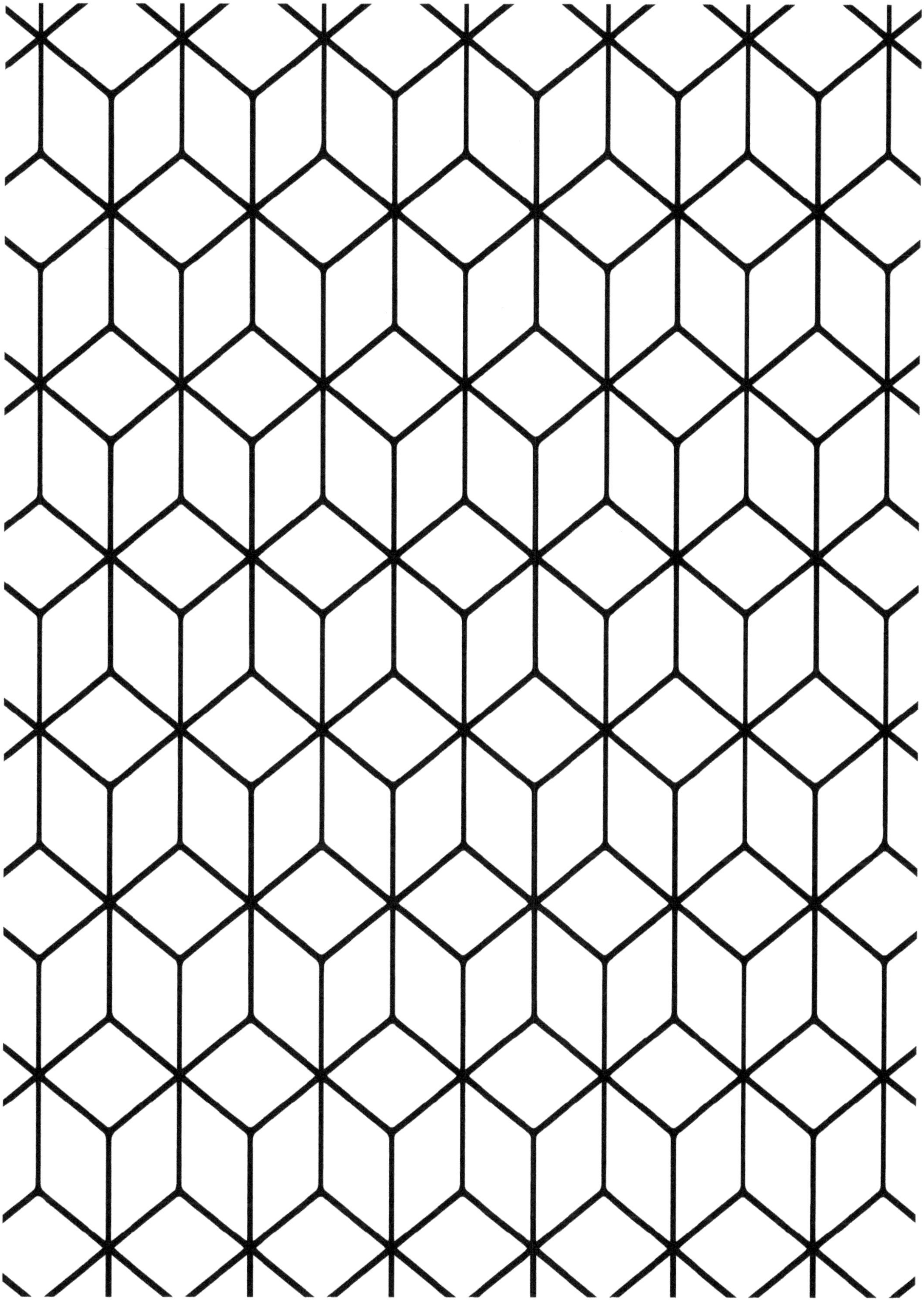

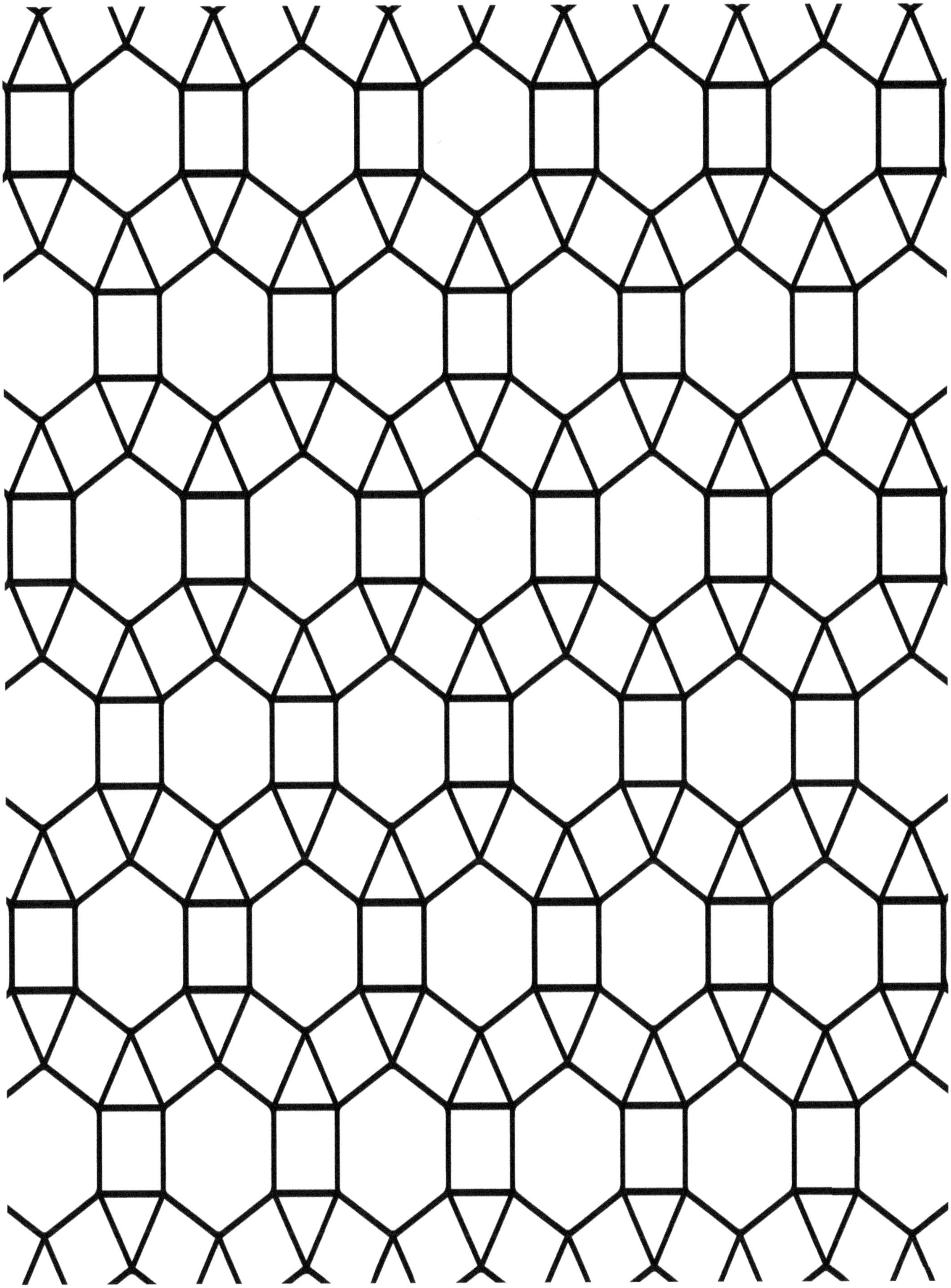

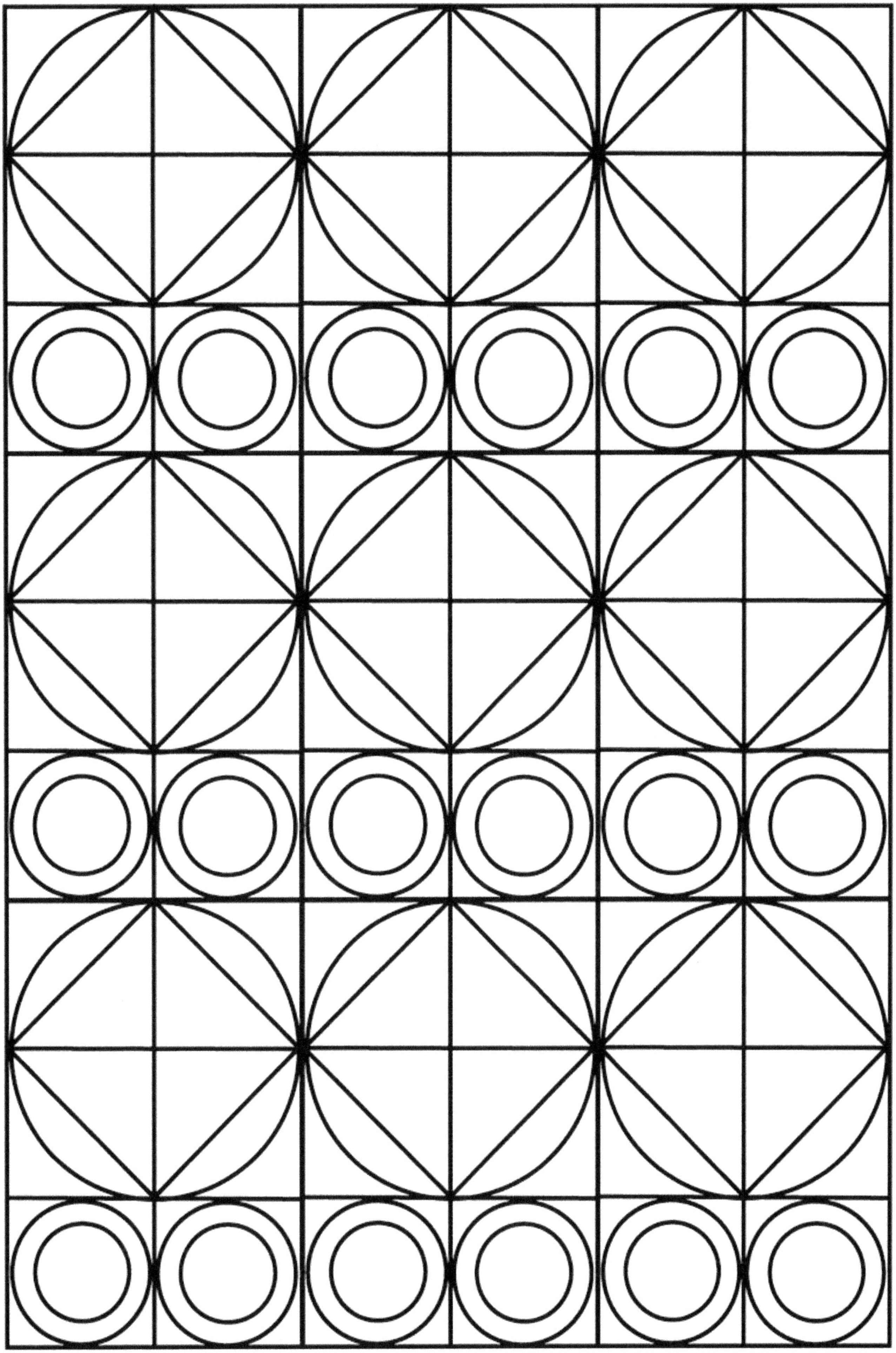

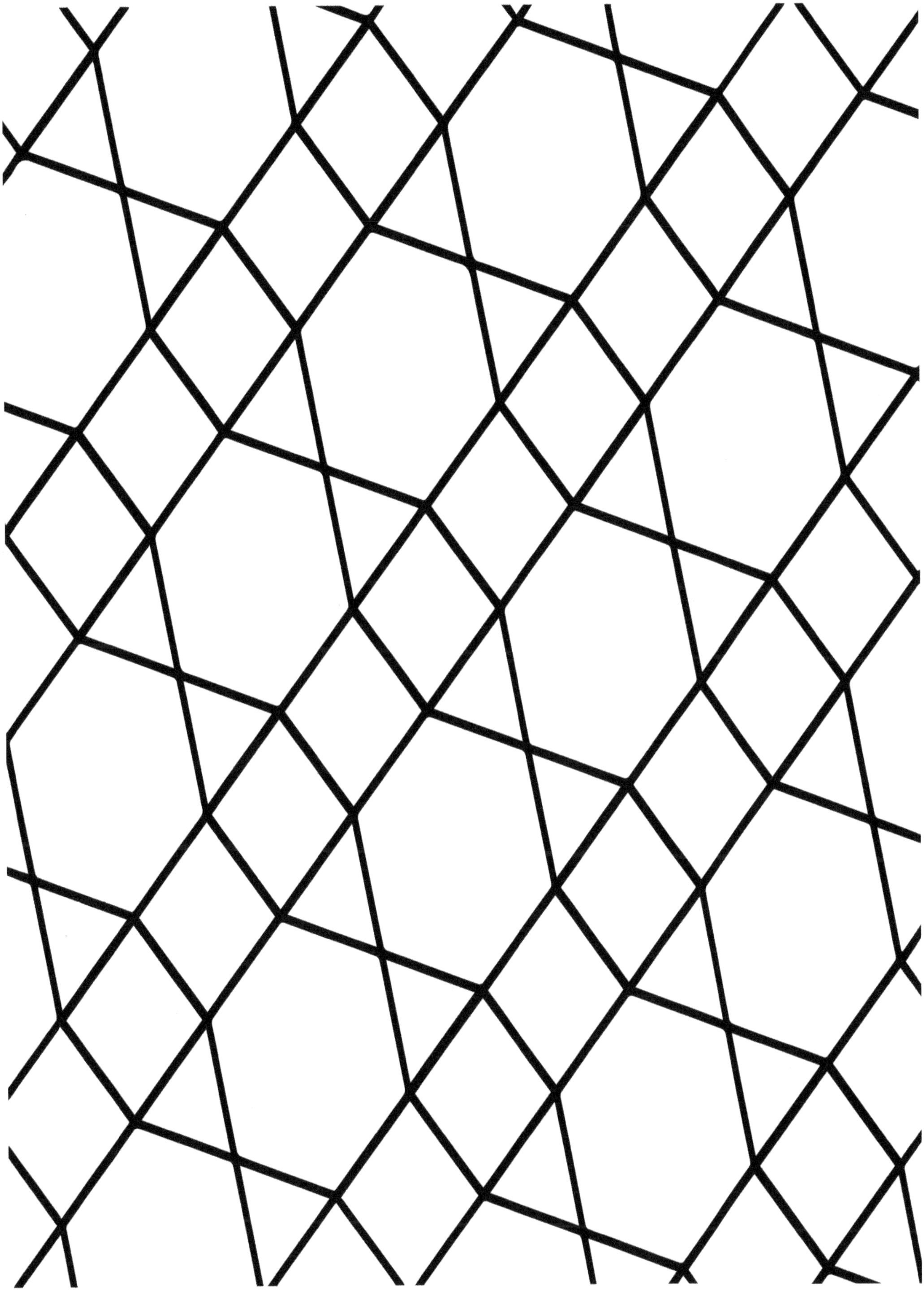

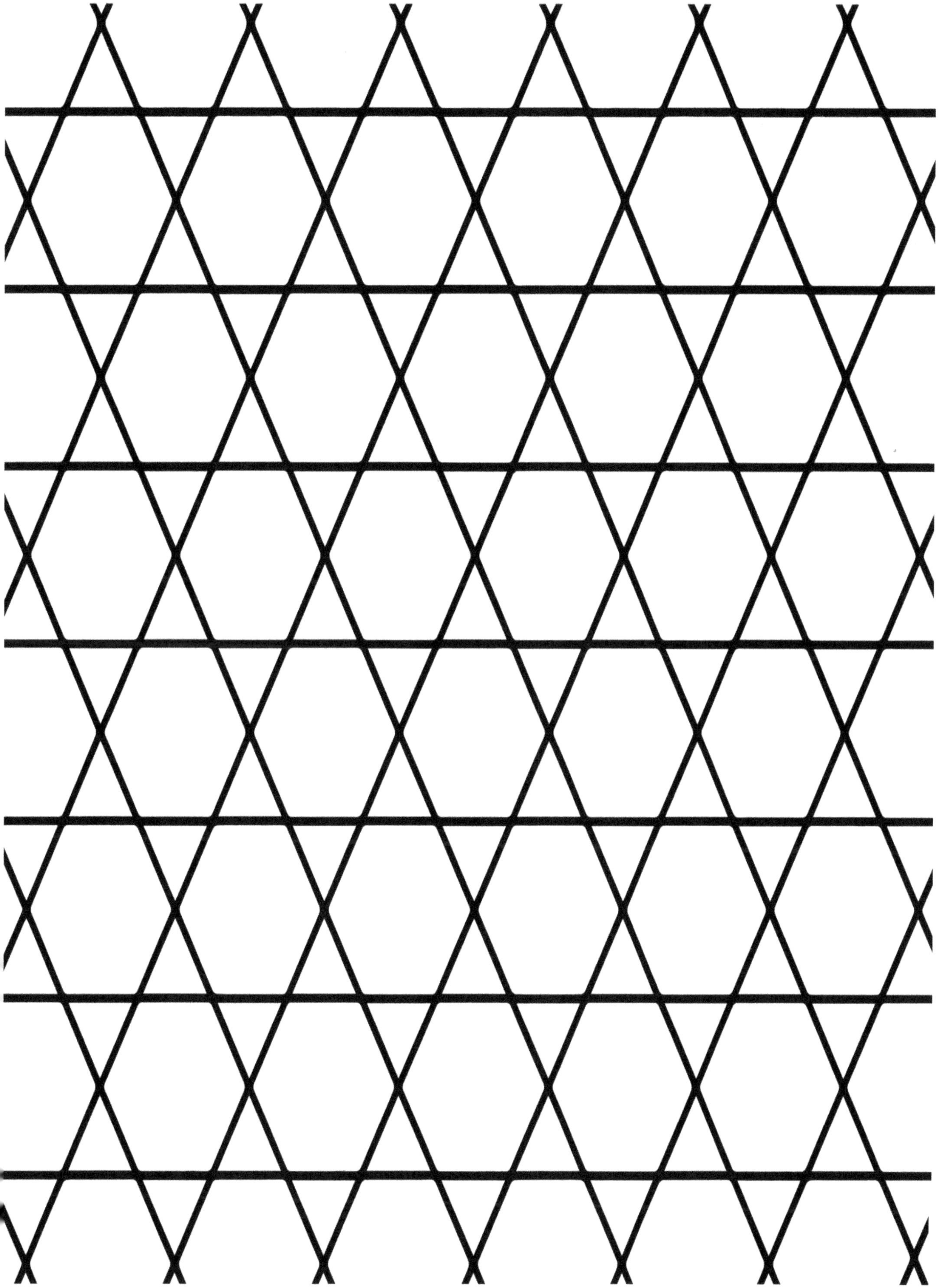

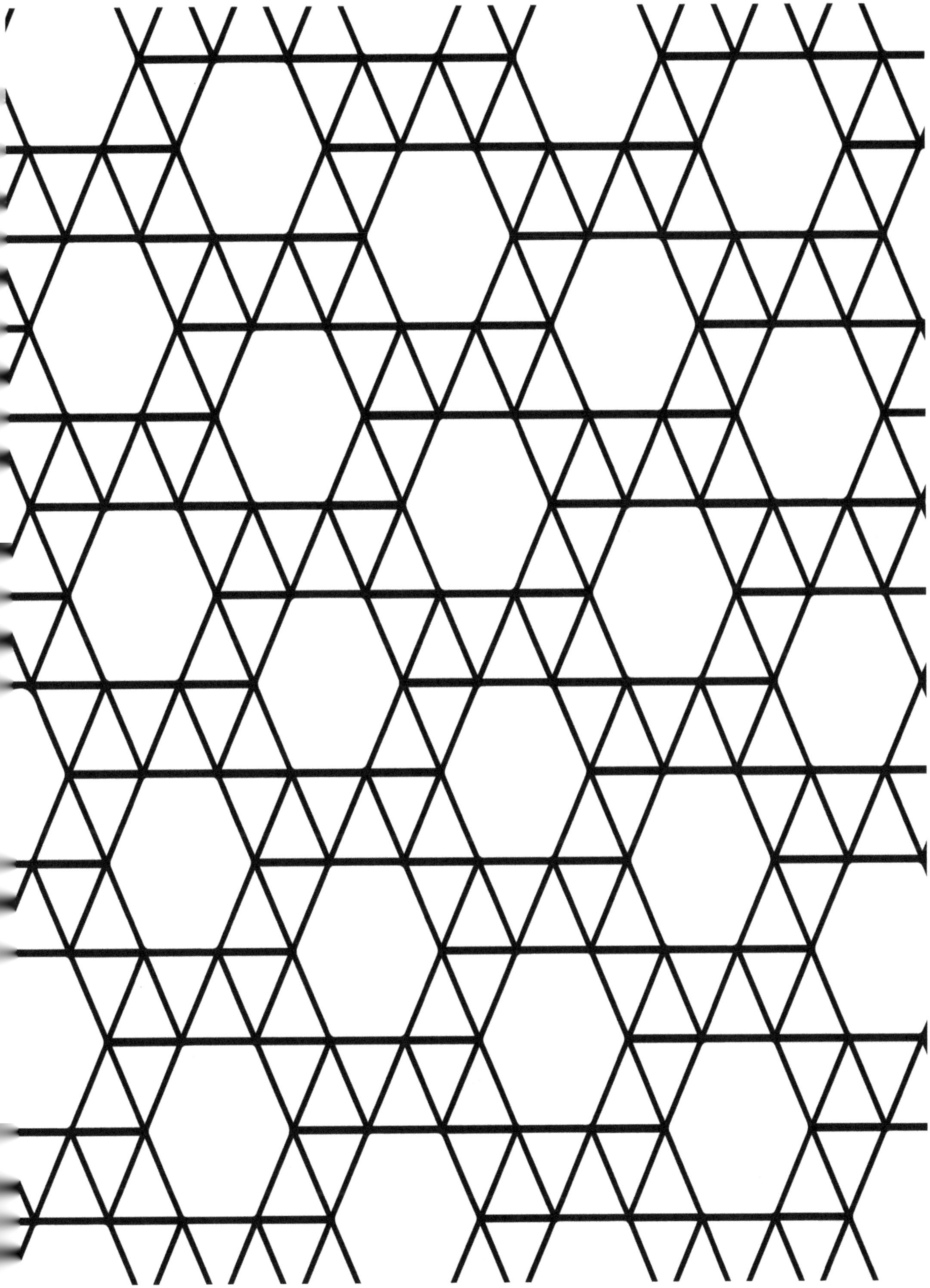

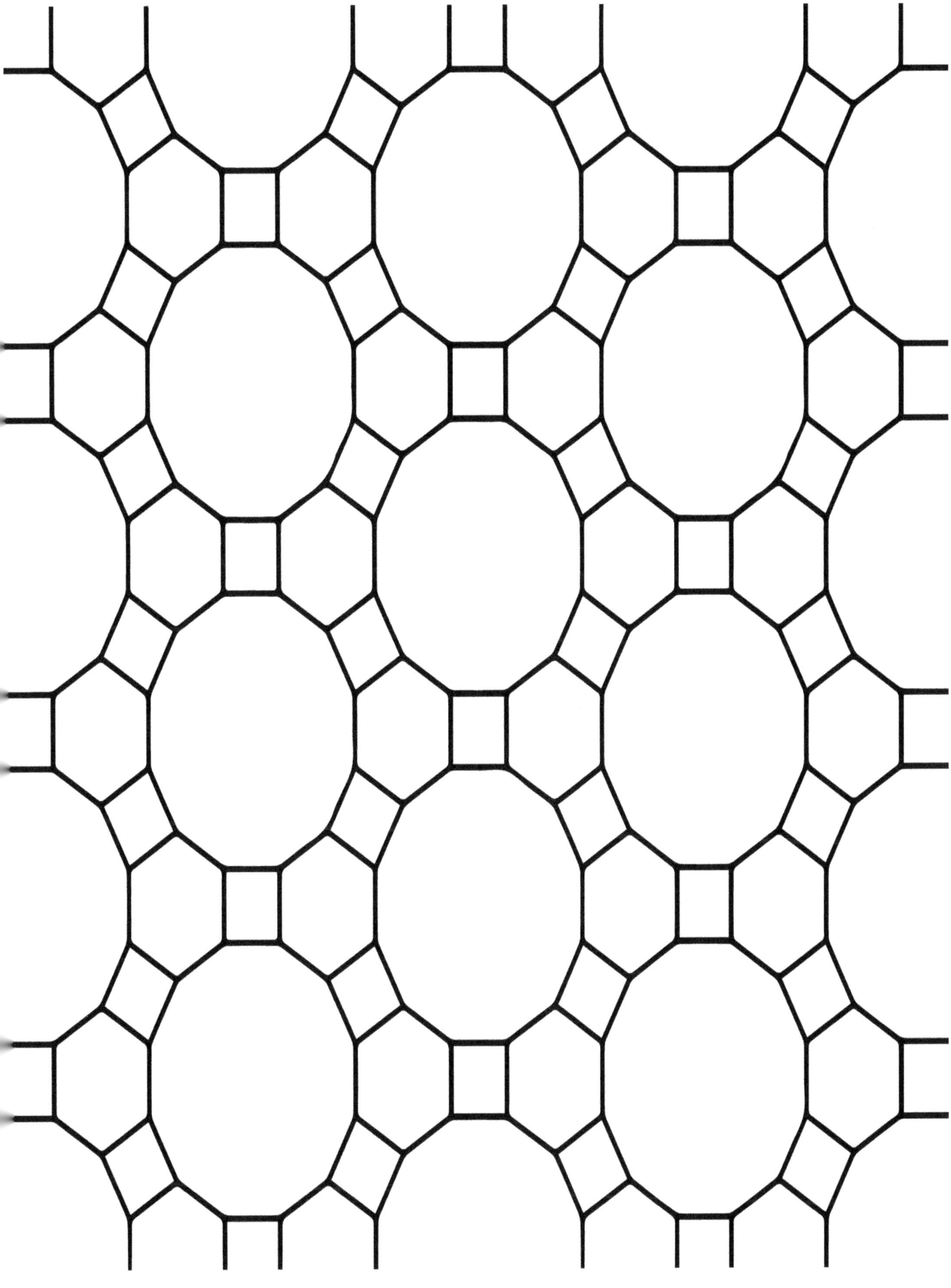

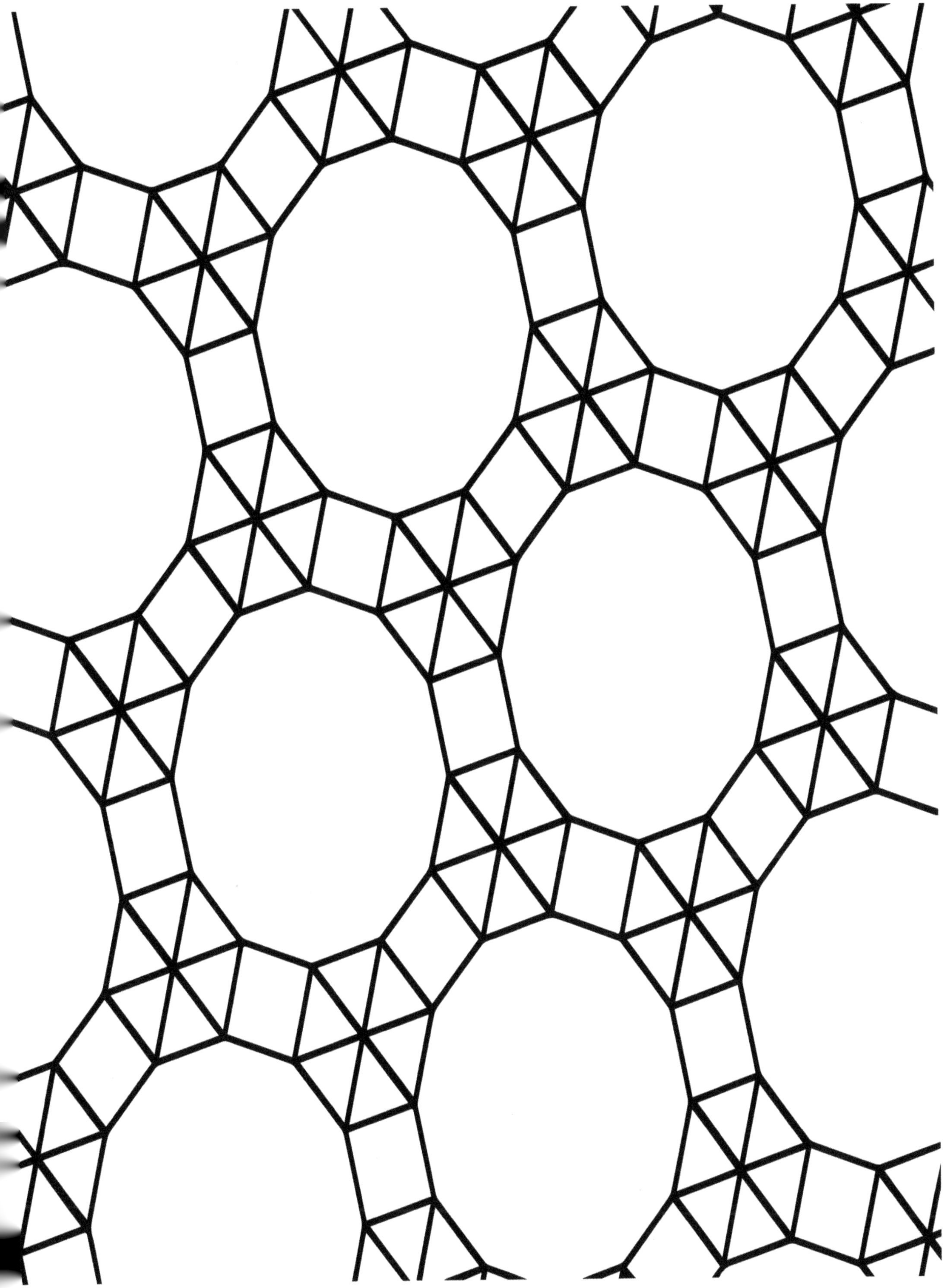

CPSIA information can be obtained
at www.ICGtesting.com
Printed in the USA
LVHW021138060121
675555LV00002B/239

9 781034 116653